Y0-BUD-955

The Alps and Alpinism

The Alps and Alpinism

edited by **Karl Lukan**

translated by **Hugh Merrick**

with an introduction by **Christian Bonington**

283 illustrations

12 in colour

Coward-McCann, Inc.
New York

Translated from the German
Alpinismus in Bildern

First American Edition 1968

Illustrations printed in Austria, text in Great Britain

Library of Congress Catalog Card Number: 68-23374

CONTENTS

FOREWORD

Karl Lukan

When in 1871 the English author Leslie Stephen published a book entitled *The Playground of Europe*, it was the Alps he meant. The 'Golden Age' of mountaineering, the name given to the years between 1855 and 1865, during which most of the great alpine peaks were climbed, was over. Many climbers of the day thought that the 'peak' in alpine climbing had been attained and even passed.

Yet in 1871 the Meije had not yet been climbed, nor the Grand or Petit Dru; important peaks in the Eastern Alps, like the Grosse Bischofsmütze, the Totenkirchl, the Kleine Zinne and the Guglia di Brenta, were still virgin. True, there were a few holiday resorts up in the mountains, but very, very few. A man of our times would either have been impressed or depressed by the silence which lay upon the Playground of Europe.

In 1913 Alfred Steinitzer published a book called *Der Alpinismus in Bildern* (A Picture-book of Mountaineering), intended as 'a survey of the development of mountaineering itself and, further, of those areas in which mountaineering can best be described pictorially'. How much it is exposed to the march of time and its changes is shown by the pictures of the 'modern mountaineering' of the period in which it was published, changes which Steinitzer, moreover, viewed with great disfavour. 'With regard to climbing in particular,' he wrote, 'modern means of transport and the activities of the Clubs have to such an extent facilitated travel among the Alps that it is even possible to reach a large number of high summits with comparatively little trouble and without the slightest danger. This has resulted in all the Eastern and part of the Western Alps being yearly overrun by a swelling flood of trippers, who disport themselves all over the mountains; for this kind of activity is, for them, the best form of sport they can find to provide them with a few moments of the health of which their daily occupations have deprived them. They all flock to the mountains for recuperation, so as not to "put on weight" or to reduce the year's accumulated adipose tissue in the least painful and most fashionable manner, to "get into training", as they mostly—and in scientific error—call it. Great as may be the influence of the whole sporting movement on personal and national health, these people can certainly no longer be classed as mountaineers.'

Today, people are still arguing about what is, or is not, genuine mountaineering. But today the Alps have in fact become the Playground of Europe, with a winter as well as a summer season. The fact that they are there, that they have been comprehensively explored and exploited, that one can climb them and ski on them, seems obvious and it does not occur to us that this was not always so.

When in 1741 two Englishmen, William Wyndham and Richard Pococke, set out from Geneva for Chamonix at the foot of Mont Blanc, they travelled armed to the teeth. Long after that, climbing ventures were still described as expeditions. The sketches brought back from them show peaks of terrifying shape, but that is how they looked to men at that time, men who approached them in a more simple-minded fashion. As late as the mid-nineteenth century, steps were being cut in ice-slopes with a woodman's axe. The 'rock-climbing experts' at the start of our own century performed their impressive achievements with equipment which would arouse a slight shudder in the climber of today. Yes, once upon a time everything was different.

Even in ancient days the Alps were never simply a barren, uninhabited region, and so the people who lived among them must, perforce or of their own volition, have climbed mountains; however, we know next to nothing about their exploits. On the other hand, the touristic conquest of the Alps by mountaineers, their transformation into Europe's Playground, has a well-known history. It would be possible to relate that story; but it can be more convincingly retold in pictures—and that is exactly what this book sets out to do.

Even then, back in 1913, Steinitzer, whose book was to inspire this one, deplored the 'drastic limitations' imposed on him by the rich mass of material at his disposal from which to select his pictures. Since then more than five decades of alpine activity have passed to swell the material available, and so our choice of what to use has given us an even greater headache.

For the final compilation of this book, the editors' and publishers' thanks are due not only to our contributors and the photographers, publishers, museums and institutions named overleaf, but also to the many unnamed helpers who gave us invaluable assistance out of pure interest in a book about mountains, whose pages are actively devoted to bygone things, in order to make the present more intelligible.

The Dent du Géant. The Giant's Tooth (opposite) is a spectacular pillar of rock in the Mont Blanc group. Moreover it is a 'Four Thousander' (13,100 ft or over) with an exciting climbing history. After the failure of every attempt to climb the Giant's Tooth in its lower third, British and Italian climbers arrived with a cannon in 1878. The idea was to fire a rope over the top and then use it as a fixed rope for the ascent; but the mountain winds frustrated the experiment. Four years later, the Sella brothers and the brothers Maquinaz finally succeeded in getting to the top. Preparatory measures akin to those of today's Grade VI ventures preceded the climb; wooden wedges were hammered into the rock, ladders fixed, ropes laid on. Was this victory, or not? The party had only climbed the subsidiary summit (13,152 ft). Now, the real summit-needle, rising beyond a notch, is all of 13 feet higher. It was climbed a month later by British climbers. Thereupon a furious and lengthy argument developed as to who had really made the first ascent of the Giant's Tooth. The photograph opposite shows the subsidiary summit as seen from the true one. The notch between the two presents no special technical difficulties. In 1900 Heinrich Pfannl, Thomas Maischberger and Franz Zimmer climbed the tooth 'free'—that is, without any artificial aids. Pfannl's verdict: 'Everyone enjoys climbing with pleasure or in fear, according to his lights.'

ACKNOWLEDGMENTS

Gustav Abel, Salzburg: 113, 114; Alpines Museum, Bern: 1, 6, 7, 15, 19, 20, 64, 71, 103, 104, 115, 180, 181, 187, 211, 218; Amanshauser, Salzburg: 149; Bergverlag Rudolf Rother, Munich: 24, 145, 168; Bildarchiv der Österreichischen Nationalbibliothek, Vienna: 8, 9, 13, 25, 30, 32, 35, 98, 101, 118, 158, 159, 161, 163, 166, 169, 170, 193, 194, 236–9, *p. 171*; Sepp Brunhuber, Vienna: 88, 176; Dieter Drescher, Meran: 38; Mario Fantin, Bologna: 74, 76, 182; Foto Fetzer, Bad Ragaz: 2; Wenzel Fischer, Garmisch-Partenkirchen: 119, 143; Collection Walther Flaig, Bludenz: 17; H. Frischauf, Innsbruck: 152; Hannes Gasser, Innsbruck: 18, 37, 105, 106; Hans Gerner, Simbach am Inn: 151; Foto Ghedina, Cortina d'Ampezzo: 21–3, 89–92, 110, 214; Jürgen Gorter, Munich: 240; Graphic Collection of the University Library, Erlangen: 43; Anton Hämmerle, Lustenau: 107; Haus der Natur, Salzburg: 10–12; Heering Verlag, Munich: 51, 56, 58, 77, 97, 184, 185, 216, 217; Toni Hiebeler, Munich: 59, 61, 84, 120; Historisches Bildarchiv Lolo Handke, Bad Berneck: 100, 164; Istituto di fotografia alpina 'V. Sella', Biella: 52, 212, 213, 219; Bahnen der Jungfrau-Region, Interlaken: 172; Eduard Kargel, Villach: 226; Klepper-Haus, Vienna: *p. 118*; Toni Kohler, Lustenau: 225; Karl Kohler, Vienna: 128, 175, 205, 220, 229, *p. 165*; Hans Kremslehner, Vienna: 153; Kunsthistorisches Museum, Vienna: 188; Robert Löbl, Bad Tölz/Obb.: 165; Friederike Lukan, Vienna: colour plates on *pp. 10, 19, 45, 49*; Archiv Maiwald, Munich: 171, 173, *pp. 50, 51, 56* (*right*); Peter Mangutsch, Innsbruck: 222; Wilhelm Maresch, Bad Goisern: 227; Archiv Erwin Mehl, Weidling/Vienna: 122, 123, 129, 132, 133, *pp. 109* (*right*), *110*; Ing. Meisinger, Vienna: 147; Karl Meusburger, Hirschegg: 230; Adolf Mokrejs, Vienna: 102, 232, colour plate on *p. 47*; Heinz Müller-Brunke, Grassau i. Chiemgau: 223; Walter Nowak, Vienna: 148, 154; Office National Suisse du Tourisme, Zürich: 14, 26, 34, 41, 42, 47, 60, 63, 73, 78, 99, 142, 144, 146, 162, 167, 174, 183, *p. 109* (*left*), *120*; Österreichische Galerie, Vienna: 36; Leopold Pahitsch, Vienna: 223; Pawlata, Vienna: 150; Foto Pedrotti, Trient: 37, 234, 235; Herbert Raditschnig, Salzburg: 83; Peter Reisser, Vienna: 3; Andreas Schandert, Staudach: 224; Hans Schmied, Munich: 108; Collection Fritz Schmitt, Munich: 5, 27, 28, 39, 44, 46, 54, 147, 177, 189, 190, 192, 199, 203, 208–10, *p. 143*, colour plate on *p. 149*; Archiv Schroll, Vienna: 45, 49, 50, 53, 57, 62, 79, 86, 111, 131, 134, 196, 201, 202, 204, colour plate on *p. 145*; P. Tairraz, Chamonix: 55, 85, 109, 121; Erich Vejvar, Maria Enzersdorf/Vienna: 228; Bradford Washburn, Cambridge/Mass.: 75, 231; Wiener Kriegsarchiv, Vienna: 130; Wolf Jürgen Winkler, Frankfurt/M.: 68, 94, 155–7, 186.

Reproductions from books:
Alpin-Journal, 1895: 90; *Anzeiger für Schweizerische Altertumskunde*: *p. 41*; Fritz Benesch, *Bergfahrten in den Grödner Dolomiten*, 1899: 221; H. Berlepsch, *Die Alpen in Natur- und Lebensbildern*, 1860: 33; *Die Besteigung der Jungfrau durch Agassiz und Gefährten*, 1842: *p. 54*; Severino Casara, *Arrampicati libere sulle Dolomiti*: 48; C. T. Dent, *Mountaineering*, 1892: 16, 65, 81; *Deutsche Alpenzeitung*: 116, 206; Joseph Enzensperger, *Ein Bergsteigerleben*: 178, 179; Arnold Fanck, *Wunder des Schneeschuhs*, 1925: 137–41; A. Fendrich, *Der Alpinist*, 1911: *p. 52* (*left*); Egid Filek, *Gustav Jahn*: 195; Will Grohmann, *E. L. Kirchner*, 1958: 207; B. Hacquet, *Mineralogisch-botanische Lustreise*: *p. 20*; F. J. Hugi, *Naturhistorische Alpenreise*, 1830: 40; Fritz Kasparek, *Vom Peilstein zur Eiger-Nordwand*: 82; Heinz Köhn, *Erich Heckel*, 1959: 197; Ignaz von Kürsinger, *Der Grossvenediger*, 1843: *p. 55*; Hubert Mumelter, *Bergfibel*: 117; Fridtjof Nansen, *Across Greenland on Snow-shoes* 1891: 136; *Der Naturfreund*, 1904: *p. 175*; *Die Österreichisch-Ungarische Monarchie in Wort und Bild*, 1889: 31, *p. 41*; *Österreichische Alpenzeitung*, 1884: 67, 87; *The Pioneers of the Alps*, 1887: 96; *Revista del Club Alpino Italiano*, 1936: *p. 52* (*above*); J. J. Scheuchzer, *Itinera per Helvetiae alpinas regiones*: 4; Heinrich Schwarz, *Salzburg und das Salzkammergut*, 1926: 200, *p. 18*; Alfred Steinitzer, *Der Alpinismus In Bildern*: 69, 70, *pp. 53* (*left*), *99*; Gaston Tissandier, *Les Merveilles de la Photographie*, 1876: 215; Edward Whymper, 1872: 66, 93, 95, *p. 56* (*left*); Friedrich Winkler, *Dürers Zeichnungen*, Vol. III, 1936: 191; *Der Winter*, 1923: *p. 98*; Theodor Wundt, *Das Matterhorn und seine Geschichte*: 72; Matthias Zdarsky, *Alpine Skifahr-Technik*, 1908: 124–7; *Zeitschrift des Deutschen und Österreichischen Alpenvereins*, 1902: 112, 135; Emil Zsigmondy, *Die Gefahren der Alpen*, 1911: *p. 48* (*below centre and right*); *Zweitausend Jahre Kunst in der Schweiz*, 1940: 198.

INTRODUCTION

Christian Bonington

The shapes of mountains change little over a few hundred years. A glacier recedes a few feet, a rock-fall imperceptibly alters the shape of a face, seracs shift, but the mountains themselves, massive and inviolable, remain the same—in shape but not in mood. A mere two hundred years ago, the summits of the Alps were untouched; a few passes had become trade routes or even passages for armies, the lower slopes and a few glaciers had been explored by chamois and crystal hunters, but the peaks themselves remained mysterious, their terror symbolized in the prints and pictures of the day.

Today, it is all changed; every ridge and face in the Alps has been climbed, *téléphérique* cables festoon the Vallée Blanche in the very heart of the Mont Blanc Massif and helicopters, like angry insects, buzz amongst the peaks. On a fine day, over a hundred climbers and their guides might jostle up the Matterhorn—300 in the day is the record—while even on the steepest faces, in good weather there are often queues.

And yet in spite of the crowds and the steady encroachment of man and his machines, the Alps retain a mystery. You might have spent the night jammed in a hut with a hundred other tourists and climbers, but the dawn start, when the frozen snow crisps underfoot, when the mountains are jagged black silhouettes against a paling sky, has the same magic it has ever held. The mountains, when clutched by cloud and storm, seem as empty and savage as they must have been before the birth of man. But beyond that, it is still possible to find places in the Alps which have not yet become popular, or perhaps have passed out of fashion. It is fortunate that people are sheeplike, flocking to the popular resorts and queueing up the well-known climbs, whether they be *voies normales* or big name routes like the North Wall of the Eiger. As a result you can still have an entire valley to yourself in the Dauphiné or Engadine, or even be the only party on the south side of Mont Blanc, while on the north, parties are plodding in their dozens on a well-marked trail.

To me, one of the great joys of mountaineering is its violence of contrast and this is perhaps the secret of the Alps' continuing attraction, and why it is the world's perfect mountain playground. The mountains, grouped in a compact bow, stretching from the Mediterranean to the Adriatic, are easily accessible to any climber in Europe. They contain every kind of rock from mouldering tombstones of Dolomite limestone to rich brown turrets of Chamonix granite. You can plod to the summit of a four-thousand-metre dome of snow, climb and scramble up some airy ridge for hours on end in a poetry of unceasing movement, or spend days stitched to a sheer rock wall trying to solve the current last great problem of the Alps. At the end of the climb is the delicious contrast of the good life in the valley. A *chateaubriant* or, for that matter, a big plate of spaghetti tastes better than it ever did before and a hot bath is a precious luxury. To me Alpinism is a form of physical LSD, of heightened sensation that at its climax reaches euphoria. It is totally addictive and the withdrawal symptoms, if I am denied my climbing, are painfully strong.

To avoid generalization I should like to focus on a single climb that gave me everything that I would ever ask from Alpinism.

The climb was the Right Hand Pillar of Brouillard, a virgin monolith of rock standing guard over the head of the Brouillard Glacier on the south side of Mont Blanc. Being unclimbed, it had all the attraction of the unknown and, more than that, it was set in one of the greatest and least accessible faces in the Alps. The south side of Mont Blanc is not like the North Wall of the Eiger; it does not tower like a stage in the vertical over the auditorium of the valley. It does not lend itself to tight melodrama that the rest of the world can watch, for it is a huge complex of sprawling ridges and chaotic glaciers, where granite fingers clutch at the sky and huge seracs can topple without being noticed. The climber on the south side of Mont Blanc is quickly lost in its vast complexity; no one bothers about his progress or could watch it, even if they wanted to. If he gets into trouble he can expect no one's help but his own. To me this is one of the greatest attractions of climbing, to be with one other climber, in whom I have complete confidence, and then to pit my knowledge and experience against the mountain. Perhaps the ultimate is to go into the mountains on one's own, like Walter Bonatti on the north face of the Matterhorn, or Michel Darbeallay on the North Wall of the Eiger, but I know that I have not that sort of courage; I am not completely self-sufficient and, quite apart from the risk, I get too much pleasure from sharing the experience to want to go it alone. At the same time, though, I avoid going in a party bigger than two; if there are too many people one loses some of the adventure and, on a practical level, the more people there are the slower the party becomes.

On the Right Hand Pillar of Brouillard I had one companion, Rusty Bailey, a twenty-four-year-old Rhodesian. We had already made one attempt on the Pillar but had been forced to retreat, through having insufficient climbing aids. We left the valley for our second attempt in the late afternoon. The Val Veni coils round the southern flank of Mont Blanc, hiding road and camp sites in a dark forest of pine. The path up to the Monzino hut winds steeply from the forest through deep grass and up rocky walls, to the accompaniment of the maniac buzz of flies and the shrieks of a few tourists dangling from the fixed ropes that safeguard the path. The hut itself is almost a disappointment; brand new, lavishly furnished and more like a country hotel than a mountain hut, it is yet another mark of man's steady infiltration into the mountains. I could not help remembering with regret its predecessor, the Gamba hut, a ramshackle wooden cabin with a single cavernous room lined with big communal bunks, and a tiny cubbyhole for the crotchety old guardian, a retired guide. The place was always dark and full of wood smoke, but you could buy a bottle of rough Chianti, and the guardian would heat up your supper over the fire. The old hut was part of the mountains; the night's stay, however cramped and uncomfortable, built up to the crescendo of excitement of the morrow's climb. There is a romance in Alpinism that is too easily lost in the big modern huts that are replacing the old cabins.

But when we left the hut at midnight, all the tension of an early start was there: that feeling of slight foreboding. Was it too warm? Would the weather hold? How about those clouds? And then as we plodded in the glistening pool of light cast by the headtorches, fears vanished in the rhythm of our movement and thrill of anticipation. To reach the Pillars of Brouillard we had to follow a ridge that sprawls down from the south face of Mont Blanc, straddling the icy chaos of the Freney and Brouillard glaciers. The first 1,500 feet was up a treadmill of scree that never seemed to end. By the time we had reached the top, the dark had paled to a watery grey; we were no longer in the safe-seeming little world of torchlight, but could see the grey shapes of seracs on the glacier below and the piled mass of the mountain above. Tattered cloud clung to the forked peak of the Aiguille Noire de Peuterey; the previous day it had towered over us, but now it lay below, dwarfed by the immensity of Mont Blanc.

In front of us stretched a gangway of steeply sloping snow. We paused in the half-light to take off headtorches and looked at each other expectantly, each waiting for the other to produce the food. I think we realized at the same instant that we had left it behind. Recrimination followed, each blaming the other, but then we began to see the funny side of it, and it all ended in helpless laughter. A careful search showed that we had half a dozen tea bags, a packet of sugar and a bag of almonds. We should have turned back, but could not bear the thought of another retreat and decided to press on. It seemed worth the risk, for with a bit of luck we should be able to get near the top that day and over Mont Blanc the next.

We were now committed to the climb. Crampons bit into the hard snow; I could enjoy the rhythm of my muscles, the knowledge of my own fitness. A jet, drawing its trail across the sky far above, somehow emphasized our isolation.

We reached the foot of the Pillar as the first rays of the sun lit the rock a warm rich brown, releasing us from the drab cold of the glacier. We quickly passed our previous high point, and reached new ground. To me this is the very essence of climbing—to choose and pick one's way up a stretch of rock where no one has ever been before. On our over-explored, over-crowded planet it is difficult to find anywhere that is truly unknown, but the climber can do this even today. It doesn't matter that the ridge to the right was climbed many years before, that the mountain itself was first ascended at the end of the eighteenth century. We were pioneering up our own little feature, were getting much the same kind of satisfaction that Edward Whymper must have received when he worked out his route up the Matterhorn.

The only possible line seemed to be up a smooth groove that soared up the face of the pillar into a belt of overhangs. It was my turn to lead and it was one of the most perfect pitches I have ever climbed, the line was so simple, the holds so sparse: just the rounded edge of the crack for clutching fingers, rugosities on the granite for toes.

There was no room for mistakes; if my foot had slipped, I could never have held myself with my hands—there just wasn't enough to hold on to. And yet this is climbing at its best, where you measure your own judgment against the chances of a fall, perhaps death itself. There is an absolute concentration; nothing exists except the few feet of rock ahead. It is a supreme combination of mental and physical co-ordination, all set in slow motion. Ten minutes can slip past unnoticed in a couple of carefully calculated moves. There is none of the lightning judgment of the high pole vaulter or exhibition gymnast.

The climb went on—each of us taking his turn to lead. Out in front one didn't notice the passing of time, but waiting below, there was time to worry, time to notice the huge anvils of cumulo-nimbus build up over the foothills to the south.

We were nearly at the top of the Pillar when it began to snow. At first I hardly noticed it, for I was out in front and could think only of climbing those last few feet to the top. But then as the rock became slippery underfoot and hands became numb, I realized that I could never make it. We had no choice but to bivouac.

There was barely a ledge, just a small niche and a gently sloping slab. We hammered pitons into the rock and tied ourselves into a cat's-cradle of rope. In the meantime, it had begun to snow in earnest, filling the air with white, rushing down the rock in powdery torrents. We had been on the go for over sixteen hours; I just wanted to curl up in the warm and go to sleep, but first we had to make our bivouac and escape from the dangerous embrace of the snow, for as quickly as we brushed it from our clothes, it covered them again. Eventually we managed to drop the bivvy sack over our heads—it's like a large bag with small airholes at the end of it. Inside it felt almost womblike, safe from the holocaust without.

But we still had to prepare for the night, get into down gear, put on long wool underpants—all while sliding down the slab, in the clammy confines of the sack. It was a matter of endless patience and care. If we dropped a boot, or even a crampon, it could mean our lives.

There was no question of lying down; we sat crouched on the slab, taking it in turns to lean on each other. From time to time we made a brew of tea—a few handfuls of snow from outside, the gas cooker held in the lap. The heat of the burner spread through the bivvy sack, but so also did the condensation from the steam. After a few minutes the burner would fade out—there just wasn't enough oxygen inside the sack to keep it going. It was easy enough to open a corner of the sack, but with fresh air came the cold—pervasive, insinuating, crawling up our legs, around our backs, till teeth chattered, helpless to do otherwise.

And then it started to thunder; the rock around us hummed and the bivouac sack crackled with high-tension electricity; a brilliant flash was followed instantaneously by the crack of sound. It was like being plugged into a lightning conductor. Wind hammered at the thin fabric of the sack and the snow poured down the rock in a flood, building behind us, slowly forcing us out from our ledge. And yet we were not frightened, but felt a strange fatalism, were even comfortable and relaxed, in spite of the thunder, cold and our cramped position. The bivvy sack seemed a tiny haven of safety in a world gone mad; we even dozed off through part of the night.

It's the morning that takes the effort; stretching cramped limbs, struggling with frozen boots, searching for climbing equipment in the all-pervasive snow. We were tempted to sit the storm out, but we had no food, and who could tell how long it would last? The rope was frozen into a wirelike hawser and had tied itself into a series of knots that frozen hands could barely cope with. From the very start one had to approach each task with a dogged patience, working methodically and slowly, with no thought to spare for the bigger issues of how we were to get all the way back to safety.

It took a couple of hours just to pack the rucksacks and get the rope ready for the long retreat. I had dreaded it all night, but now that it was upon us, there was a strange kind of exhilaration in having survived the storm. The snow poured over us, around us, at times engulfed us, but we were warm in our shells of down clothing and proofed nylon, and felt secure in our own ability.

The entire day was spent in slowly working our way back to safety, sliding down iced ropes, and wading through thigh-deep snow, but that night we were down in the valley. We had failed to make the first ascent of the Right Hand Pillar of Brouillard, stopping only a hundred feet below its top, but we had no sense of failure. It wasn't just a feeling of relief at being alive, for we had never felt that our lives were in danger, but in the storm we had contended with forces more violent that we had faced before, and the satisfaction that I gained from this was even greater than straightforward success could have ever been.

For me, this climb combined everything that I love in Alpinism, the beauty and loneliness of a huge face, the physical pleasure of cramponing over frozen snow and climbing warm holdless rock, the struggle with elemental force, and finally the glorious contrast, a superb four-course meal and the warmth of a dry sleeping bag.

Although techniques have changed, I am sure these basic motives for climbing are no different now from what they were over a hundred years ago; but it is sad how often an older generation has misunderstood the younger, when in fact they have so much in common. Immediately before the war, the pundits of the Old School, led in large measure by the Alpine Club, thundered against the methods used by a new generation of Continental climbers. Colonel Strutt, as President of the Alpine Club, stated in 1938: 'The Eigerwand continues to be an obsession for the mentally deranged of almost every nation. He who first succeeds may rest assured that he has accomplished the most imbecile variant since mountaineering began.' And then in 1966, the very people whom Colonel Strutt had castigated in their turn attacked the methods of a new generation of climbers on the ascent of the Eiger Direct, because they made extensive use of fixed ropes and returned to the hotel at Kleine Scheidegg for rests during the climb. And yet they were innovating new methods to solve a mountaineering problem in exactly the same way that the pioneer of the 'thirties had done before them. No doubt, as I get older, I shall find it difficult to sympathize with the motives and techniques of yet another generation of climbers, and so it goes on.

Every sport has its pioneers, the men who innovate and inevitably stir up controversy. In the Alps the leading climbers are already finding it difficult to pioneer to the full, as more and more routes are put up, interlacing every wall with climbs. As a result, the pioneers of today are having to look further afield, to the Andes and Himalayas, where there are still many hundreds of unclimbed peaks and faces. Having climbed most of the difficult Alpine climbs in the summer, they now try them in winter, or straighten out existing lines with direct plumb line ascents, just to find something new.

But the average mountaineer with limited summer holidays can still find complete satisfaction in the Alps. He does not mind if others have been before him; in fact he prefers it, for he feels safer following a guide-book description. The young climber on his first Alpine holiday gets as much excitement and pleasure from walking up the ordinary route on Mont Blanc, as the expert might from climbing the North Wall of the Eiger. It does not matter at what level one climbs, how long and difficult the route—the joy of Alpinism is absolute.

LIFE IN THE ALPS

Karl Lukan

The Drachenloch is in Switzerland, in the Drachenberg near Vättis, at a height of 8,000 feet. Its entrance is accessible only by way of rock-cliffs, graded by today's scale of climbing difficulty as 1 – (= easy). Between 1917 and 1923, while the cave was being excavated, a kind of stone box was uncovered about six feet below ground; in it were seven well-preserved skulls of cave-bears. This discovery aroused great excitement. It was clear that the skulls had been placed in the box, in their day, by the human beings who lived there, the Neanderthal men—as part of a ritual, in the view of the archaeologists who dug them up. From this it followed that the Neanderthal man was by no means the primitive creature he had till then been held to be. Furthermore, these discoveries high up in the mountains established the fact that the Alps were one of his stamping-grounds, and that he must have engaged in modest mountaineering feats when out hunting among them.

In 1929 the antiquarian Leonhard Franz wrote: 'That race, of whose speech and origin we remain ignorant, whose blood no longer survives in a single descendant, but whose tough, hazardous life is revealed by these discoveries, are thus established as the first high-mountaineers, the first mountain hunters, the first users of the Alps; perhaps someone will be found, in this monument-crazy age, to honour the memory of those unknown climbers with a memorial stone.'

'The horrid Alps'—as the historian Livy called them—were seen by other Romans, too, as nothing but the home of winter, thunderstorms and tempests; not one of them visited the region unless he had to. Even in the Middle Ages, the plainsman became familiar with the Alps only if compelled to visit, or even to cross them. This created a false impression, widely held right up to our own century, that in ancient times the Alps were a blank on the map of Europe. The truth is that men lived in the Alps even before the last great ice-age and again directly after it, in other words long before the dawn of history—hunters, herdsmen, farmers, miners and traders. In face of the discoveries in the Hallstatt cemetery, we cannot avoid the conclusion that, in the first century BC, there were even a few men of substance living in the valley there.

The first people to come to Hallstatt, about four and a half thousand years ago, were hunters, drawn there by the great concentration of game around its salt-bearing springs. When the waters evaporated, man began to gather salt for his own use. Later, tunnels were driven into the hillside and great blocks of salt recovered. The Romans, too, were at Hallstatt, and the salt-mountain became a rich source of income for the later lords of the land. For some centuries past the salt has been retrieved by 'washing' it out of the mountain. The brine thus acquired is piped to boiling-houses, where it is evaporated in iron pans. In about 1600 these drying-sheds were moved from Hallstatt to the well-wooded area around Ebensee, with its greater sufficiency of fuel. The brine was brought there by a 20-mile pipe-line.

Other commodities won from the Alps were copper, iron, lead, silver and gold. Indeed, it was gold from the Alps which precipitated a financial crisis in Italy in the second century BC. When large quantities of gold, so easily recoverable that it was only necessary to dig down two feet to uncover nuggets as large as beans, were found in the land of the

Noric Tauern, people came up from Italy to share in the work. Two months later, gold in Italy had fallen to a third of its previous value and, not unnaturally, the Tauern people got less in return. So the Italians drove them out and established a monopoly of gold from the Tauern. How tough a business this recovery of gold from the high Alps was to become later on, is revealed in an 1889 report, which runs: 'The team of 40 miners forms a tiny colony, devotedly carrying on its arduous labours in summer and winter at a height of about 7,000 feet. The dangers and hardships these miners have to face in their fight with the elements are beyond description.'

'Everything in the Alps is frozen fast . . .', wrote Silius Italicus (AD *c.* 20–100), a poet. Albrecht von Haller was a poet too, but in his poem, 'The Alps', published in 1729, he described the mountain scene in terms of an aesthetic experience:

When the sun's beams put parting mists to flight,
Wiping cloud tears from every weeping place,
Each living thing shines, painted with new light
That gilds each leaf, refreshes Nature's face.

The reality—the life of herdsmen, hunters, woodmen and farmers in the Alps—had little or nothing in common with pictures drawn by the poets, even when they present dramatic scenes in words carrying great conviction, as in Claudius Claudianus' (born *c.* AD 375) account of Stilicho's crossing of the Splügen Pass: 'Many a warrior was frozen stiff, as had he gazed on the Gorgon's face, many were deep-engulfed in great masses of snow; many a waggon and its team plunged into the abyss like a foundering ship, now a mountain collapsed under the burden of sliding ice, while the mild Föhn-wind made unsafe each foothold, in that it undermined the ground beneath. Through such a frozen wilderness of ice did Stilicho proceed. No beaker of wine to bring solace here, no ear of corn. Fortune was it here to taste some garnered morsel without laying aside of arms; down-laden with his dripping cloak, the rider beat his shivering steed to warmth. No soft bed here for the weary; for when the sombre darkness of the night did fall, then crept the soldier into some cavern where lurked the fear of wild beasts, or slept in some poor shepherd's hut, his shield a pillow for his head. Pale-faced gazeth the shepherd on the mighty intruder, and the mother of the peasant family displays in wonder to her grime-covered brood the wondrous figure, the like of which she had never seen before.' Even today many a lowlander is horror-struck by his first contact with the mountain world, and shepherds' huts with grubby children in them exist now, as they did in days gone by.

The ancient historians record that Alpine cattle were small but yielded much milk. Cheese was made, corn harvested and, on the southern fringes, men made wine. Wood was cut and marketed. Other commodities sold or bartered for other goods were: animal skins, honey, wax, pitch, resinous wood, curative herbs. Besides these, there were the minerals already mentioned. The dwellers in the Alps have added only one source of income in the course of all the centuries: foreign tourism!

So, we know that men could sustain life in the Alps as herdsmen, farmers or hunters. As far back as the end of the second century AD there were missionaries at work in the Alps and the great monasteries founded later were an important factor in the spread of culture in the area. 'Never would he, who hath only beheld the Alps from afar, guess that beneath the eternal snow and on the slopes of those mountains, upon which everlasting winter and never-melted masses of snow do freeze, may be encountered paradise-places, fresh with the breath of health and life.' So wrote Felix Fabri, the pilgrim-preacher from Ulm, who on his missionary journeys in 1480 and 1483 came to know the Alps at first hand.

The healing springs of the Alps have been in use for four thousand years, as was revealed when in 1907 the prehistoric aspect of the curative spring at St Moritz was established. People already visited Pfäffers and Gastein for water-cures in the Middle Ages; and the visitors to the baths at Leukerbad during the Renaissance are known to have lived a *dolce vita*, owing to which they were ultimately blamed for a terrific storm, considered by others to be Heaven's retribution for their goings-on.

It was possible to exist in the Alps, though the life of those living among them was never the kind of idyll the young Rousseaus and, later, the nineteenth-century holiday visitors imagined it. Even if the inhabitants never had to combat dragons and griffins, as the legends and even the early books maintained, hunting among the mountains claimed numerous victims. Avalanches, landslides, floods engulfed men as they slept, nor is the phenomenon less prevalent today. The mountain-dweller's life is a hazardous life. And so it was suggested, as late as the seventeenth century, that the Alps had earlier been inhabited only by strong giants, on the premise that the 'mountains were made for the people who lived among them, and the people to match the mountains.' (Wagner, *Historia naturalis Helvetiae curiosa.*)

It was Guido Rey (1861–1935) who, in his remarkable reconstruction of the Val Tournache at the foot of the Matterhorn, provided a unique description of the lives of the alpine people as they might be imagined before the foreigner came to the Alps: 'I can see in my mind's eye one of those romantic travellers of the first half of the century, come from afar to venture among the Alps, in the days when they were known only through the studies of a few men of science, or the vision of certain poets. I can see him climbing for the first time up the lonely valley path, his mind filled with the dream of an idyllic peace, of a free and primitive life, awakened in him by the writings of Haller and Rousseau; and already he dreams that the happiness of the pastoral life is about to be revealed to him.

Wolf Huber, Traunkirchen and the Traunstein: pen-and-ink drawing, 1519.

The bridge at Pondel, at the foot of the Gran Paradiso, is the most impressive piece of Roman architecture in the Alps. Built in 3 BC, its arch, 50 ft wide, spans the Grand Eyvia torrent, more than 150 ft below.

'But when he enters the village street, he sees that things are not as the poet portrayed them; a sense of something forbidding, almost akin to terror, is conveyed by the sight of the low, dark houses, huddled one against the other for purposes of mutual protection against the cold and of resistance to the shock of the winds; the garments of the hill-folk are poor and ragged; their forbidding faces are never lit up by a smile; their life is a hard one, as is that of all things which live and grow in those high places, and man's fate up there is like that of the pines, which fill the fissures of the rocks with their deep-burrowing roots, suck up the nourishment from the barren soil, and grow in serried groups strong enough to stand the weight of the snows, and live till the hurricane uproots them or the avalanche sweeps them away; or else die slowly of old age when the sap of life is in them no more. No man notices that there is a pine the less in the forest, or a cross the more in the little cemetery.

'Perhaps the troubles and the worries that pertain to town life are not apparent in the mountains, but there is instead a sort of stupor, of dull, continuous suffering. The summer is short: the rest of the year is winter, and the mountain dweller patiently awaits in his closed stable the sun's return; the time for harvest is short, and the work of gathering it in is heavy, the placid joys of labour do not seem to brighten men's lives in these high places, but hopeless resignation to fate shapes their course.'[1]

[1] Guido Rey, *The Matterhorn*, Chap. II, in J. E. C. Eaton's beautiful translation.

Hacquet's mineralogisch=botanische Lustreise von dem Berg Terglou in Krain, zu dem Berg Glockner in Tyrol, im Jahr 1779 und 81

(*Hacquet's Mineralogical-botanical Pleasure-tour, from the Triglav Mountain in Carniola to the Glockner Mountain in Tyrol, in* 1779–81.)

The writer of this work, from which the picture on the left was taken, says about the Grossglockner, 'I never saw so high a peak as sharp as this one.' The picture certainly shows a terribly sharp peak. An asterisk marks 'the eternal ice on its midnight side'. Belsazar Hacquet, an explorer and natural-historian, firmly believed that 'the proper precautions' would take him to the unclimbed Glockner's summit 'so as to measure it'. However, he advised strongly against any such undertaking, unless armed with shotguns. 'At such heights,' he wrote, 'one often has to fight with a very powerful enemy, the great birds of prey that swoop on one and strike one to earth or into the abyss with their mighty wings. I know not whether they mistake one for chamois or for some other thing; suffice it that they rule undisputed over such high places. Whosoever sets foot in their realms runs great dangers from them, be he not possessed of fire-arms.'

The Schreckhorn, too (13,386 ft), appears as a terribly sharp peak on the coloured engraving facing this page. When Peter Birmann (1758–1844), a landscape-painter from Basel, produced his engraving, no one had even given a thought to climbing this savage peak.

The first human being in the Alps was Neanderthal man. On Plate 2 a white circle marks the entrance of the Drachenloch (8,000 ft) in the rocky face of the Drachenberg (eastern Switzerland); this cave was probably inhabited by Neanderthal man, certainly visited by him on his hunting expeditions after cave-bears. The picture is an impressive reminder of the high alpine landscape in which primitive man moved about. Many present-day inhabitants of the hills still believe in prehistoric monsters like dragons and griffins, supposed to live in crannies in the mountains: meetings with the latter have been reported even in this century! In his *Itinera per Helvetiae alpinas regiones*, published in 1723, the Zurich scientist Johann Jakob Scheuchzer even went as far as to categorize them precisely as winged, wingless, without feet and many-footed; he also provided pictures of some of these monsters (Plate 4).

Forty thousand rock-pictures on Monte Bego (French Alps) confirm that the inhabitants of the Alps were offering sacrifices to a heavenly power as long ago as the second century BC, at altitudes from 6,000 to 8,000 ft. Plate 3 shows the so-called 'Wizard', a man holding above his head in each hand a bronze dagger – one of the most impressive drawings found at this pilgrimage place of long ago in the high Alps.

3

◄ 2

4

There were made-up roads in the Alps before Roman times. The Romans transformed these existing tracks into the Roman roads, of which traces are to be seen all over the Alps. Then there are the famous Roman columns on the Julier Pass (Plate 5 shows them in an engraving by Johann Meyer in the mid-18th century). These columns are not, as so often claimed, milestones, but the dissected pieces of a single column of marmoreal stone, which probably supported the statue of a god. A similar column, preserved in its entirety, still stands on the Little St Bernard Pass.

Between 1736 and 1741 the Cantons of Valais and Bern were engaged on the construction of the rocky road over the 7,640-ft Gemmi Pass (Plate 7). H. Berlepsch wrote in 1860: 'This is one of the most perilous tracks anywhere in the Alps. A deep, gloomy rift splits the rocks of the mountain-face from bottom to top; in it a rock-path, climbing from one, as it were, "landing" to another directly above it, was constructed by the provision of artificial walls or by blasting. Every shout, every spoken word evokes a resounding echo, as in the empty aisles of some great church. At the same time, the downward view, over breast-high protecting walls, onto the rocky chaos below, is horrid indeed.' The daring ladder-way from Leuck to Albinnen was also built in the 18th century (Plate 6).

◀ 5 ▲ 6 7 ▶

Peace and war in the mountains. Hannibal led his army across the Alps, supposedly losing 20,000 men in the process. Plate 8 depicts 'the toilsome and remarkable march of the Imperial army over the Tyrolean and Old Noric Alps in the year 1701'; Plate 9, the transport of a gun on the Italian alpine front in 1918. There is a remarkable similarity between the two pictures. A soldier's life in the mountains, no matter at what period, has always been hard and arduous.

Plate 10 shows mountain-troops on a peaceful mission: the recovery of the seven giant crystals from the north face of the Eiskögele in the Hohe Tauern with the aid of a cable-ropeway built by sappers. This, the greatest find of crystals yet made in the Alps, weighed altogether 30 cwt, one crystal alone, 3 ft 7 ins tall and 7 ft in girth, weighing 11 cwt. The discovery was made by two climbers in 1965. Plate 11 shows one of them, Peter Meilinger, who fell to his death a year later, with his find. In September 1966 the crystals were recovered and transported to Salzburg's 'Haus der Natur' by helicopter.

▲ 11
◂ 8 ◂ 10
◂ 9 ▼ 12

Eternal ice. Plate 16 shows the 'Wilderwurm' Glacier. This picture in Dent's *Mountaineering* (1892) supports the suggestion that glaciers shaped like snakes may well have led to the dragon-myths of alpine inhabitants.

In a 19th-century lithograph (Plate 15) the Zermatt Glacier, too, looks like a gigantic monster at rest. And the summit cornice of the Gross Venediger (drawn by Friedrich Simony in 1856, Plate 13) looks as dangerous as the open gullet of a reptile. Man is very small in this marvellous world of eternal ice (Plate 14 shows Glacier 'Tables' in the Bernese Oberland).

'Eternal ice? What a misconception! It is renewed a hundred times over in its ever-moving, ever-sliding course. Not a snow-flake survives from its original state. It flutters down... it crystallizes into ice... it melts away, to float up again in the endless circuit of the waters, in whose eternal world-journey a glacier is but a moment in time, no more.' So writes Walther Flaig in his *Gletscherbuch*, published in 1938, in which he also maintains that 'the dominion of the world's glacier-ice extends over a tenth part of the firm surface of the Earth.'

◀ 13 15 ▲
◀ 14 16 ▶

Avalanches. In winter man's worst enemy in the high mountains is 'the white death'. In spite of all protection against avalanches, avalanche-warnings and avalanche danger-signs (Plate 18), the recent growth of winter-sports has led to a steady increase in the number of avalanche disasters. Plate 17 shows one of the most famous representations of an avalanche from times gone by. It is an illustration from David Herrliberger's *Topographie der Eydgenossenschaft* (1773) and shows one of the 'great lumps of snow rolled together into a huge ball, which crash down into the valleys and depths from the topmost, treacherous mountains with a furious and horrifying cracking and roaring sound.' For a long time avalanches were represented as gigantic cannon-balls, but in spite of this erroneous conception, no mistake was ever made on one point: their annihilating results!

People who nowadays get themselves borne swiftly to the heights by rail and ropeways very often know too little about the grim facts of conditions among high mountains. One of the oldest presentations of men in the wintry wilderness of the great peaks is an aquatint by C. Wolff from the *Description of a journey which was accomplished through part of the Bernese Alps in 1776* (Plate 19). We also reproduce the detail of the two climbers in this picture: two small people in a cold world of terror, a world in which every step forward is arduous beyond words.

◄ 17 ▲ 18 19 ►
20 ▼

When mountains fall. In 1860 H. Berlepsch wrote in his widely-read book, *Die Alpen in Natur- und Lebensbildern:* 'No storm on the vast ocean, when the fear of foundering gapes at the sailor from a thousand billowy graves, no eruption of a volcano flinging its fiery sheaves blazing to the skies, no conflagration sweeping through America's forest primeval can evoke a more shattering moment of terror than that in which the horrified mountain-dweller shouts to his wife, his children and his neighbours, "Run for your lives! The mountain is coming down!"'

Plate 21 shows the village of Longarone in the Piave Valley. During the night of 9 October 1963 a huge mountain-slide forced the water in a reservoir above Longarone out over the dam (Plate 22 shows the masses of earth left in the reservoir) and the resulting cataract simply swept the whole village away in a matter of seconds (Plate 23). The dam itself had held.

A photographer, whom it has unfortunately proved impossible to identify by name, showed great courage and presence of mind when, suddenly, a whole mass of rock fell from the Lalidererwand in the Karwendel with a thunderous roar (Plate 24).

21
22
23
24 ▶

Alpine animals. It was by animals that men – first the hunters, and later the herdsmen – were originally lured into the mountains.

In 1716 Scheuchzer wrote about the chamois-hunter: 'It often comes about that he goes out hunting early in the morning and either fails altogether to return or is carried home grievously hurt.' The Emperor Maximilian I, however, found hunting in the mountains his favourite recreation, even after he had lost his way on the Martinswand and been rescued by a chamois-hunter after a long time. (Plate 25 is a detail from a picture in one of the hunting and fishing books prepared for him in about 1500.) The bear-hunters often had to cope with dangerous situations (Plate 27). As late as 1860 a driver had to scare a bear off the Engadine road with a crack of his whip.

In Plate 26 the peaceful occupation of herding sheep to the far side of the Valaisian glaciers is shown. A sudden break in the weather would mean disaster for many such flocks.

The St Bernard dog was at one time the only means of rescue for many a traveller overtaken by bad weather while crossing the high passes. These animals had an amazing 'nose', and almost a special sense, for tracking those who had lost their way or had been buried by an avalanche. How many there were can be judged by the fact that, a century ago, the St Bernard Hospice gave shelter to some 20,000 souls a year; if further evidence be needed one should remember how few days free from fog and snow there are on these heights.

◀ 25 26 ▲

27 28

▼ ▼

The worker in the Alps. The world's first pipe-line was built in the Alps – the conduit from Hallstatt to Ebensee. Plate 29 shows the 'Gosauzwang', constructed in 1757, to carry the pipes across the gorge of the Gosaubach. The remarkable feature of this functional edifice is how well it fits into the landscape. The onward transport of the salt recovered was by boat down the Traun and the Danube. The falls of the Traun near Gmunden were negotiated by a weir, the boats shooting headlong downstream – a perilous hazard for the boatmen, none of whom were swimmers! (Plate 30 is taken from the periodical *Über Land und Meer*.)

29

30

31

32

33

The woodworker, too, has always led a dangerous life. Plate 33 (from a sketch by Emil Rittmeyer) shows a woodman roping down into a ravine to release stranded driftwood; to get back he had to be hauled up on the rope. Bringing the hay down to the valley by sledge in winter, too, was more than a toboggan-ride (Plate 32 is from the same periodical as 30). The memorial-tablets are evidence of how dangerous a working-place the Alps are. Plate 31 shows the mining installation on the Rauriser Goldberg in about 1880. Even in a book designed to popularize the Austro-Hungarian monarchy, it had to be conceded that the life of the miners up there at 7,500 ft beggared description.

The Alps as a health-resort. The medicinal springs in the Alps were already in use in prehistoric times: Plate 34 shows the hot springs in the Tamina Gorge, discovered in 1038 and provided with their first bathhouse in 1242 (lithograph by Eugène Ciceri, 1859). The sick were lowered to the healing waters in a 'lift', those who suffered from giddiness having their eyes bandaged. Rousseau expressed surprise that 'baths in the health-giving air of the mountains are not one of the leading curative methods of medicine and morality.' It was not long before the Alps were in fact discovered as a resort for rest and recuperation. This produced the first close contact between the townsman and the mountain people, whose manners and morals were as foreign to him as those of any exotic tribe. Plate 35 is a lithograph by Anton Schrödl (1823–1906) showing alpine festivities on the Alp below the Dachstein, where the Gablonzer Hut now stands. A mountain beacon-fire is being lit, there is singing and wrestling, and shots are being fired into the air, while on the seesaw a young lad is teaching a lass the basic principles of fear.

34

35 ▸

The painter Heinrich Reinhold had always wanted to work where nature is at its grandest. So in 1818 he and several fellow-artists embarked on a journey to Salzburg and Berchtesgaden, one of whose results was his oilpainting of the Watzmann, reproduced opposite. In it a human being appears as a very small thing.

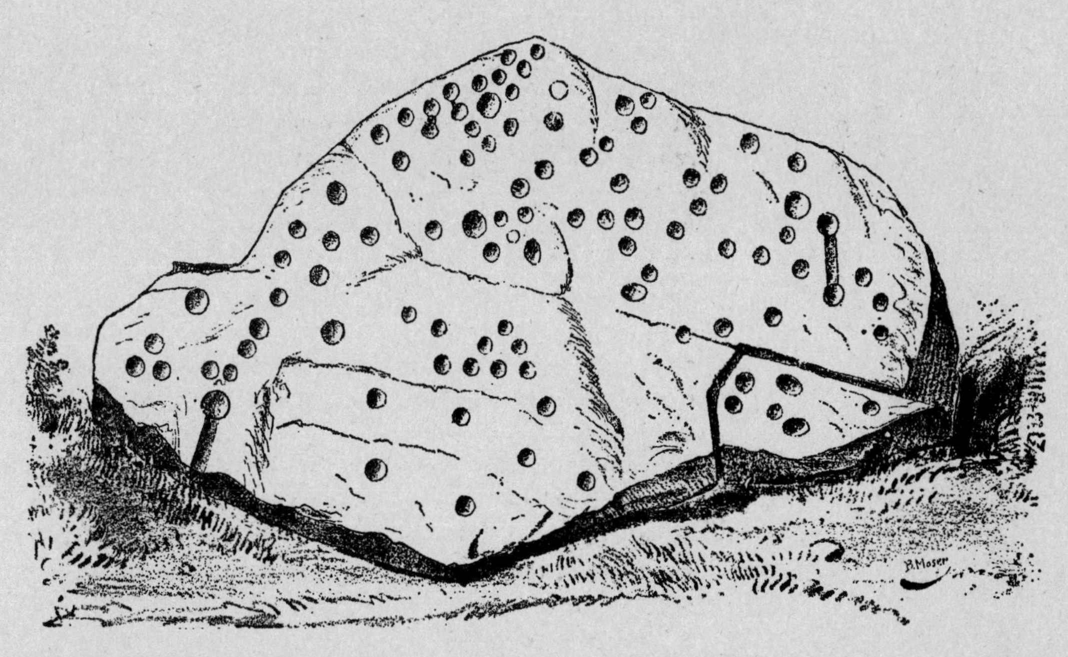

Rindstones is the name given to rocks in which prehistoric men bored small indentations, in some cases even proper troughs. They exist almost all over the world, and are found at localities and altitudes in the Alps at which the idea was long resisted that human beings could have been at home in prehistoric times. In 1870 the Swiss archaeologist Ferdinand Keller, often called the 'Schliemann of the Alps', wrote: 'They constitute an archaeological riddle which will probably never be solved.' Today it is generally accepted that these rocks belong to a fertility cult.

The Hallstatt Finds. It was in 1846 that J. G. Ramsauer, a master-miner, while sinking a shaft, came upon a skeleton. Further digging revealed a prehistoric graveyard. Between 1846 and 1864 altogether 993 graves, and 6,084 exhibits found in them, were brought to light. These articles (bronze and iron weapons, helmets, precious adornments and ordinary household utensils) are among the most important finds in Europe before the turn of the century; as a result, in 1871, Hallstatt, a small village situated deep in the mountains, was able to give its name to a whole culture (the 'Hallstatt Culture', 900 to 400 BC). The drawing on the left comes from the *Austro-Hungarian Monarchy in Text and Picture*, published in 1889. In it the artist, Hugo Charlemont, has successfully pointed the impressive contrast between the precious finds and the primeval setting in which they were discovered.

The idea that the inhabitants of the Alps in days gone by were completely insensitive to the surrounding scenery consequently persisted for a very long time. There are, however, indications that this conception was wrong, as wrong indeed as the romanticized picture of a mountain idyll, which was written round the men of the hills towards the end of last century and which has survived to this day in films, plays and television scripts. The last few decades have witnessed an intensive preoccupation with the traces left behind him by prehistoric man, rock-paintings, rindstones, footprints in rocks. There is no doubt that these are always associated with places of worship. Many of these still carry legends of devils and witches, of men under spells, or of God's wrath. However, a great number of these primitive worship-sites were later transformed into Christian shrines (holy wells, footprints now attributed to the Virgin Mary or to one or another of the Saints). There are many theories about these original places of worship.

A notable feature—as seen today—is that they are all situated in some special spot in the surrounding landscape: on top of an imposing hillock or on some prominent spur, commanding a wide view, in some impressively dark corner of the hills. So the choice of these sites would seem to confirm that the prehistoric inhabitants of the Alps already had a strong sense of the unique nature of their surroundings.

The peaks, too, famous as 'sun-dials' (the Zwölfer, the Mittagsspitz and such 'noonday' summits), were part of the mountain-dweller's ambience. And when, last century, the Val Tournache guide Jean-Antoine Carrel played such a leading part in the struggle for the Matterhorn, it was not done for money; it was 'his' mountain and he wanted to be the first man to stand on its summit.

It used to be held that, before the mountaineers came, no peak of any great height had ever been climbed by local men; and this applied equally to the high summits of the Western Alps and the more difficult ones at the Eastern end. But there are plenty of other mountains. On the Fanisalp, at a height of 8,500 feet, stands the prehistoric Fluchtburg. Does it seem unreasonable to believe that one of the herdsmen may have climbed up to the 10,000-foot Zehnerkofel rising behind it, if only to get a better view? Climbing-irons keep on turning up in graves dating from the fifth century BC. We all know that the chamois-hunters of later days were 'tough climbers'. Is it impossible for one or another of them to have climbed on beyond his chamois-range and up on to a sharp summit? True, none of them has left a cairn or his visiting-card on one. His 'heroic deed', which his friends may perhaps have wondered at and admired, was forgotten again two generations later. Such an achievement would not have found its way into a chronicle of the times, for it would not have been thought worth recording. Yet, today the belief that the past had its 'Unnamed Climber' is growing steadily. There are no traces of him; perhaps none will ever be found. Nor is the conception intended in any way to belittle the pioneers of alpine exploration. What is intended is to establish once and for all that the Alps have always been the home of human beings, not merely 'a blank in the map of Europe'.

CLIMBERS IN THE ALPS

Karl Lukan

On 8 August 1786 the first men stood on the summit of the highest mountain in the Alps, Mont Blanc. Yet, in 1854 an Englishman, John Murray, was putting on record in his *Handbook for Travellers in Switzerland, Savoy and Piedmont*, that the majority of those who climb Mont Blanc are 'of a diseased mind'. Between 1786 and 1850, seventeen summers had seen only thirty-one ascents of Mont Blanc, shared among fifty climbers, excluding their guides.

For the author of Murray's Guide everyone who climbed the mountain for other than scientific reasons had a 'diseased mind'. The very idea of climbing mountains save in the cause of science! Even in 1880 J. Doblhoff was displaying the same attitude when, in his book about Mont Blanc, he complained: 'Unfortunately, in the 93 years since Saussure's first ascent, the majority of the climbs have been purely the ventures of tourists. In place of the meteorological observations, temperature-measurements, hygrometer- and barometer-readings, pulse and breath-counts (which every layman can take) we mostly find nothing but the apparently essential emptying of a bottle of champagne or brandy and the traditional signals down to Chamonix; at the very most, someone sketches the surrounding mountain-outlines or experiments with the reverberations of shots fired into the valley.' And when Paul Güssfeldt wanted to climb Mont Blanc's Peuterey Ridge, he obtained the German Emperor's permission—for he was of his following—in these words: 'Since science demands it, you may go!' That was in 1893. So, more than a hundred years after the first ascent of Mont Blanc, its finest ridge (still one of the great alpine undertakings today) was climbed for the first time 'in the name of science'. Güssfeldt also made the first ascent of Piz Bernina's Biancograt, a ridge which nowadays ten or even twenty parties do on a fine summer's morning. But, in his view, his climb ought never to be repeated, since his ascent had 'once and for all established the way in which Pizzo Bianco and Piz Bernina were connected to one another, and no second climb was required to confirm the information.'

Nonetheless, there had always been people who climbed mountains simply because they enjoyed it—such as the Swiss naturalist Konrad Gessner, who wrote to a friend in 1541: 'What rapture must fill the mind of him who looks in wonder at the vastness of these great mountain ranges and lifts his head, as it were, into the bosom of the clouds!'

Today, mountaineers take photographs. The travellers of yesterday sketched. If you could not sketch very well, you 'described' the landscape to an artist, who finished the commissioned picture from your indications. If the artist had never seen a high mountain, inaccuracies, not to say exaggerations, were likely. We get the same exaggerations today, when people execute drawings of outer space, as described by astronauts, though they themselves were never in outer space. The coloured lithographs reproduced in this volume from W. Pitschner's 1860 book about Mont Blanc are examples of such imaginary mountain landscapes. In the one entitled *Ice-masses in the Early-morning Alpine Glow*, the colour of the sky (half way between day and night) and the red of the 'glow' on the mountain's summit-structure in the dawn-light were as 'commissioned' by the artist's patron as the pictures themselves. In several other pictures, on the other hand, one peak or another appears so incredibly sharp just because the observer saw it like that; for, when we look at that kind of a picture of the mountains, we must never forget the relationship between the early mountaineer and his mountain. For him it was a new world, in which he moved, inspired by scientific or adventurous motives, but with a certain degree of fear at heart. As Sir Charles Fellowes declared after climbing Mont Blanc in 1827: 'If I could persuade a friend of mine to give up the idea of attempting what we have done and endured, I should credit myself with having saved his life!'

There is a fairly comprehensive pictorial documentation from the early days of mountaineering and, if its artistic value is not great, there can be no doubt about its social and historical importance. Moreover, it provides valuable evidence on the development of those two increasingly important factors in the growth of mountaineering—technical skill and equipment.

EQUIPMENT: Climbing boots at first had a smooth sole. On steep slopes, on snow and on ice, 'climbing irons' were strapped over the boot. The knight Theuerdank (hero of the Emperor Maximilian's famous work, published in 1517) almost fell to his death while on a hunting expedition 'for that the snow had balled up between his foot-irons'. Saussure climbed Mont Blanc in top-boots, later providing himself with 'glacier-nails', which could be strapped on to their heels. In 1799, when Goethe visited the Mer de Glace, he felt very insecure on the 'slippery surface' for, as he wrote: 'We were equipped neither with foot-irons nor even nailed boots, and worse still, through much walking, our heels had become rounded down and smooth.' In spite of that, Goethe climbed down on his leather soles from the Montanvers to the Mer de Glace and everyone who knows this descent (on which several deaths had already occurred) will regard this mountaineering feat of his with due respect. In pictures of journeys undertaken in 1828 and 1829 in the Bernese Oberland by the Swiss naturalist Hugi, one can detect men in shoes, and since these plates were authorized by members of the expeditions, there can be no doubt that 'Half-shoe tourists' took part in the first ascent of the Finsteraarhorn. Eventually it became common practice to wear nailed climbing-boots, even on purely rock-climbing routes. The 'Kletterschuh' with a sole of plaited hemp was not discovered till the 'nineties of the last century. Up till then difficult pitches were climbed barefoot or in socks, after the manner of the game-hunters.

The early mountaineers in the Alps climbed in ordinary city suits. Frock-coats of cloth, and trousers were worn, as also a top-hat and, later, big caps. For the most part they wore plenty of underwear and a few warm scarves were tied round their necks. Climbing must have been pretty laborious in such clothes. Veils were worn as a protection against the sun; talc or gunpowder was also rubbed into their faces.

Spare clothes and provisions (cold meat, cheese and dry bread) were carried in shoulder-panniers, later in canisters. Not till the mid-nineteenth century did the rucksack become common usage on big climbs.

The first ascent of the north face of Montasch in the Julian Alps was undertaken in the year 1902 by Julius Kugy and some companions. When in 1910 the Alpine Section at Villach celebrated its fortieth anniversary, the Committee decided 'instead of noisy festivities, which have only an ephemeral value, and in place of an expensive publication, to institute a commemorative alpine project, to be at once a monument to the Section and a joy and aid to innumerable climbers.' So it was decided to convert Kugy's route up the Montasch north face into a safeguarded rock-path.

To achieve this, '300 yards of steel cable with wooden grips and 870 iron stakes were necessary, and 500 steps had to be cut into the rock. In many places the work could only be completed by allowing the workers to swing clear of the face on a rope, to which a wooden bar was attached to serve as a seat. The transport of the ropes and stakes to the upper part of the face demanded the most exhausting efforts. The stakes weighed a total of 11 cwt, the ropes half as much, and this immense burden had to be lifted piecemeal to the heights.' (J. Aichinger.)

It seems almost miraculous to anyone who ascends this 'Villach Way' that it took three masons only two months to fashion the whole route up the face. The photograph opposite was taken above the Bergschrund. A projecting nose of frozen snow has overlaid the safeguarding aids and the pitch has to be turned on smooth rock, involving Grade IV climbing skill. In spite of all the safeguards an ascent of the 'Villach Way' still demands a safe performer on rock. And there are many mountaineers who would be turned back by the exceedingly wide Bergschrund at the foot of the face, the crossing of which is in itself quite an adventure.

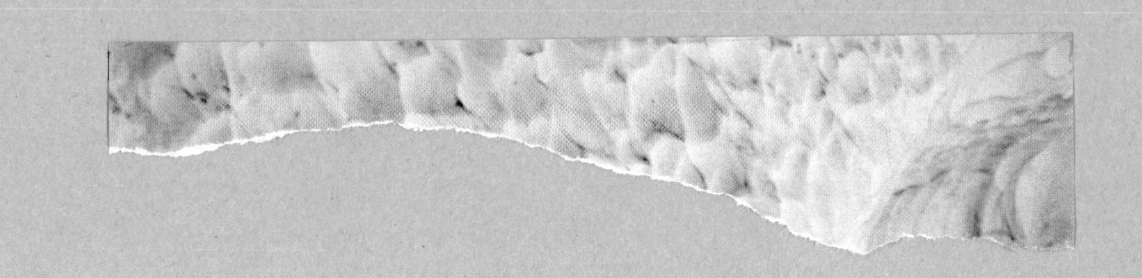

ALPINE TECHNIQUE: The alpine rod, without which nobody would approach the mountains till well into the nineteenth century, is to be seen in pictures as far back as the Renaissance. It was often ten to twelve feet long and it was used—as the pole today in the Pole Vault—to accomplish the most hazardous leaps across clefts in the rocks. Later on, at dangerous passages, the guides built a kind of bannister of these rods to comfort nervous patrons. A guide would hold either end of the rod, while the 'Herr' clung to its middle. Ladders were carried for the crossing of crevasses. The ice-axe was at first unknown. One of the guides would take an ordinary woodman's axe along for step-cutting. Still later it became the practice to tie the axe to a shaft and the guide would proceed at the head of his party with this lethal weapon clutched in his fist. The ice-axe finally resulted from an inquiry by members of the Alpine Club in 1864 as to what would be the most efficient form of instrument for its special purpose.

Ropes were taken along on mountain expeditions by crystal-hunters in very ancient days. The pioneer climbers took them along too, but very rarely tied on to them! These cords (often actually mere string) were used for rescuing anyone who fell into a crevasse; and if anyone got stuck on a cliff they threw the string to him so that he could hang on to it. It was not till about 1830 that climbers began to tie themselves to a rope. When at last they did so, as many as five or six would go on a single 100-foot rope; everyone climbed simultaneously, there was little belaying, and they had the rope tied once round their waists. That there were not more accidents speaks volumes for the skill of the guides of the day. Only a really great mountaineer like Leslie Stephen recognized this fact and wrote about it: 'And here let me make one remark, to save repetition in the following pages. I utterly repudiate the doctrine that alpine travellers are or ought to be the heroes of alpine adventures. The true way at least to describe all my alpine ascents is that Michel or Anderegg or Lauener succeeded in performing a feat requiring skill, strength and courage, the difficulty of which was much increased by the difficulty of taking with him his knapsack and his employer. If any passages in the succeeding pages convey the impression that I claim any credit except that of following better men than myself with decent ability, I disavow them in advance and do penance for them in my heart.'[1]

The first great achievements of guideless climbers ushered in a new chapter in the history of alpine climbing. More people started to climb. The desire to stand on a peak untrodden by the foot of man led their steps to lower but more difficult mountains. And as the difficulty increased the danger, so the greater danger demanded a decisive improvement in alpine techniques.

But many loved the danger for itself. The great solo-climber Hermann von Barth shouted after his climbing-staff as it went hurtling into the gulf: 'Who climbs with me must be prepared to die!' Eugen Guido Lammer, too, was consumed with 'an unquenchable thirst for mortal peril'. It was a time when men were wallowing in Wagner's heroic operas, when Nietzsche's Zarathustra was born and when mountaineers raved about Ernst Platz's painting *Death and the Climber*. People, of course, still went up into the mountains with the idea of staying alive!

The following sentences were penned by a great English mountaineer, C. E. Matthews, for Clinton Dent's handbook for mountaineers, *Mountaineering*, which appeared in 1892: 'We can never over-estimate what we owe to the Alps. We are indebted to them and to all their charming associations for the greatest of all blessings, friendship and health. Let anyone who has been in the great playground of Europe for twenty or thirty years try for only a moment to erase from his memory the many friends whom but for the love of mountaineering he would never have known. What terrible gaps would be left in his history, what happy recollections would be effaced, what warm sunshine would be taken out of his life! Such friendships, too, are always perpetual; the sharing in common difficulties and

[1] *The Playground of Europe*, Chap. II.

En route to the Gnifetti hut

common dangers must of necessity bring men closer together. The brightest recollections of youth or manhood form the most abiding solace of old age. But years form no barrier to the enjoyment of mountaineering. It has been conclusively proved that of all sports it is the one which can be protracted to the greatest age. It is in the mountains that our youth is renewed. Young, middle-aged, or old, we go out too often jaded and worn in body and mind, and we return invigorated, renewed, restored; fitted for the fresh labours and duties of life.' Alongside text-books of this kind on climbing technique, guide-books and maps were beginning to appear. An attempt was made to establish a scale of difficulty. And the first piton was driven into a rock-climb!

Iron stakes had for a long time been driven in by hunters on steep ground for use as foot-holds, but at first mountaineers would have nothing to do with such artificial aids. It was not till they were faced with ever-increasing difficulties that they resorted to them. 'Iron-mongery' was first used to facilitate belaying. Stones were used to knock the 'nails' in.

In the end, ring-pitons were adopted, because when a man fell off, the rope so easily slid off the piton over which it had been laid; and the rope was then threaded through them. This process was naturally time-consuming and not without its dangers, especially when climbing on steep rock without a second safety-rope. An improvement was achieved by tying the climbing-rope to the piton with a light line. The final solution of this belaying problem was the metal snap-link, first used by the Munich climber Otto Herzog in 1910, which immediately became the basic aid in an entirely new climbing technique—the mastery of vertical rock faces by means of a double rope and pitons. The argument whether the 'ironmongery' approach to face-climbing is really mountaineering continues to this day.

It was after his attempt in 1883 to climb the south face of the Dachstein with August Böhm that Carl Diener wrote: 'We do not believe that the problem of this climb will be solved before the face itself is worn away to its very base.' The face still stands, soaring to the sky: thousands of climbers have made their way up it by numerous routes worked out since that day. Diener was one of the climbing *élite* of his time; but his prophesy—like almost every prophesy about the possibilities and performances of future generations of climbers—was completely wrong.

A caricature by the alpine painter Platz, dating from 1911, shows the ghost of that great pioneer of routes in the Northern Limestone Ranges, Freiherr von Barth, looking down in scorn on a face plastered with 'nails'. The end of true mountaineering, in his view! At the time, of course, there were no such 'piton-ladders'; nowadays they exist. Yet, in spite of every prediction as to its future, climbing has not yet reached the end of the road. Men still climb mountains; only they climb them by methods widely differing from those in force a hundred, fifty or even twenty-five years ago.

The first ascent of Mont Aiguille (6,876 ft), shown opposite, was made in 1492 by Antoine de Ville and a dozen companions at the behest of his king. What a great achievement it was can only be judged by one who has stood at the foot of this huge pillar of rock. The parliamentary envoy for Grenoble, who was sent to verify the facts of the letter Antoine de Ville wrote on top of Mont Aiguille to report the success of his attempt, recorded his own reaction: 'The very aspect of this mountain is sufficient to strike fear into him who beholds it.' This envoy, Ive Levy, saw the ladders leaning against the mountain's face and, on its summit, people and three wooden crosses. Antoine de Ville invited him to come up and join him, but he declined on the grounds that he did not 'wish to challenge the Almighty'.

Unfortunately, no technical account of this climb exists. Antoine de Ville only mentions artificial aids and describes it as the most terrifying and appalling journey of his life. Ive Levy tells of ladders brought to bear on the rock. Mont Aiguille plunges on every side in extremely steep rock-faces 600 to 1,000 feet high. How many ladders were used—and how were they managed? Were they hoisted on ropes? How were the pitches between ladders mastered? It is a great pity that this so-called 'birth of extreme climbing' is shrouded in so much darkness.

The easiest way up Mont Aiguille today is by a path safeguarded by steel cables. Even then it is still accorded the second grade of technical mountaineering difficulty.

The first disaster on Mont Blanc. 'The first, and because of its particular circumstances, worst disaster, that of 20 August 1820, befell the party of Dr Hamel, the Russian naturalist. Hamel with two Oxford university dons, accompanied by the guides J. M. Couttet, Math. Balmat, Devouassoux and others, as well as by a great many porters carrying the mathematical and scientific instruments, provisions and the like, went up to the Grand Mulets on 16 or 18 August 1820. There they spent the night in the open and by nine o'clock next morning found themselves only a few hours below the summit. Hamel despatched letters by pigeon-post, while the scientists collected slates and geological samples, and made observations of the snow conditions. Suddenly the snow gave way, forming an avalanche. Hamel was dragged down by it and almost suffocated, but in the end managed to work himself free. A count showed that five men were missing. Thunderstruck by this revelation, Dornford and Henderson were on the verge of despair, only Hamel kept control of his feelings. Presently two men emerged from the depths like corpses risen on the Day of Judgment; but the other three had disappeared. Yet not permanently; for, forty-one years later (on 12 August 1861), just as Dr Forbes had predicted in 1858, parts of their bodies and clothing came to light, as did Hamel's veil. Two of the original guides, Marie Couttet and Jules Devouassoux, were still alive and recognized the relics. In 1862 Wey found further objects and a single hand below the snout of the Glacier des Bossons. In that same year Auguste Balmat met Dr Hamel, now an old man, in the British Museum, where Tyndall was showing the aged Russian around. With bated breath the guide related the story of the finds, whereon Hamel remarked quietly, almost cynically: "So Forbes and Tyndall were quite right; now the rest will come in due course; it should make a very interesting museum for the trippers." Those were the words of a man who had seen three of his comrades being swept into the abyss.'—From *Der Montblanc* by J. Doblhoff, Vienna 1880.

A mountaineering lecture in 1853. In 1851 Albert Smith of London, accompanied by four of his friends, climbed Mont Blanc. For the next six years he gave lectures on this feat at the Egyptian Hall in Piccadilly. The stage was fitted out as a Swiss châlet, in front of which was a pond, surrounded by blocks of granite and plants, with live fish in it. The walls were decorated with items of mountaineering equipment, pictures of Mont Blanc and the flags of the Swiss Cantons. In 1853 a newspaper reported: 'The Hall is filled night after night by a highly select audience, no less excited than that during the last season.' Queen Victoria was among those who heard Smith give his lecture.

Mr Erasmus Galton's hazardous ascent of Mont Blanc in 1850. As Galton himself recorded, he was not used to drawing pictures. A Mr Jewitt of Plymouth made the drawings which have been reproduced here, using rough sketches that the climber had given him.

On the way up, one of the porters carrying ladders slipped and fell head-first into a crevasse, where he remained hanging from a projecting ledge, supported by the ladder. At the bivouac, on a narrow band of the Grands Mulets, Mr Galton only had to raise his head, as he lay, to look down on the glacier 400 feet below without having to move his body. For the final ascent to the summit he stuffed his ears with paper and smeared his face with hot tallow from lighted candles. Just below the top he gradually lost consciousness and, half-blind, half-deaf, staggered onwards like a drunken man. On the summit he slipped and would have fallen to his death, had not a guide caught him at the last moment. Despite everything Mr Galton's reaction to this perilous climb was: 'Oh God, how wonderful are all Thy works!'

The extreme limit of possibility, pictured left. In 1934 Alvise Andrich and Ernani Faè made the first ascent of the north-west face of the Punta Civetta; it took them nineteen hours. In 1936 the German edition of a book called *The Uttermost on Rock* by a Venetian climber Domenico Rudatis appeared, in which the author, himself an 'extremist' on rock, author, artist, painter, mountain-photographer and film-cameraman, suggested that the climb of the Civetta's north-west face represented 'the extreme limit of possibility'. 'The unlimited development of progress is a myth or, more precisely, the capacity for wishful thinking and self-deception. Where climbing is concerned, the deception is governed by artificial aids. The mere introduction of new artificial aids can in no way extend the true frontiers of the possible, for the simple reason that every kind of climbing with known or still unknown aids induces a lessening of the bodily or psychological powers or performance.' He adds: 'Owing to this purely manual method of gaining height, climbing tends to become increasingly uniform. The purely mechanical application of sheer strength, however great it may be, can in no way be regarded as an essential manifestation of the true art of climbing.'

This sketch by Rudatis was made to illustrate an article by Ernani Faè on the first ascent of the north-west face of the Civetta, which appeared in the *Rivista del Club Alpino Italiano*, 1936.

The early days of the piton. Below centre: one of the so-called 'picture-hooks' with the rope laid over it. Below right: a climber belays himself and protects his leader by threading the rope through ring-pitons. Both pictures are taken from Zsigmondy's handbook *The Dangers of the Alps* (revised edition by Wilhelm Paulcke, 1911). In the same year A. Fendrich's climbing manual *Der Alpinist* appeared. In it a climber is shown banging a piton into the rock ('that small inseparable comrade of the rope') and he is doing it with a stone (below left)! And in that year, too, the alpine painter Ernst Platz already foresaw the piton-galleries of modern days. He portrays the ghost of that great solitary climber and explorer Hermann von Barth gazing down scornfully from Heaven on a world he no longer understands (facing page, left).

In the photograph on the right, small people swing airily in space on steel-cable rescue equipment; the Mountain Watch provided this shot during a practice rescue operation.

The Jungfrau (13,670 ft) was first climbed in 1811. The lovely white mountain, already named Jungfrau (the Virgin) in the sixteenth century and whose summit would, according to the belief of the local inhabitants, remain for ever virgin, was mastered by a rich family of Aarau merchants, the Meyers.

The head of the family, Johann Rudolf, wanted to donate to his country a new, more accurate map. The entire expenses of the survey work before the compilation of the maps (which appeared as *Der Meyersche Atlas der Schweiz*) were borne by the family. During the preparatory operations the wish was engendered to climb the Jungfrau, the most beautiful mountain in the Bernese Oberland. It was fulfilled by two sons of Johann Rudolf Meyer, accompanied by two guides from Valais. On purely scientific grounds? Hardly! For when doubts about the ascent were noised abroad, another son of Johann's repeated it in the following year to confirm his brothers' success. It was not till sixteen years later that seven inhabitants of Grindelwald made the third ascent, dragging a 20-lb rod with an iron flag fixed to it up the summit. Whereupon the Swiss government authorized the Mayor of Interlaken to reward each of the participants with a double gulden.

The Jungfrau was climbed a fourth time in 1841 and a book about the climb was published a year later, entitled *The Ascent of the Jungfrau by Agassiz and his Companions*. The above picture is a reduction of the sketch for the book's jacket. The climbers are shown positively floating among the clouds.

In 1886 the *Neue Zürcher Zeitung* announced as an April Fool's Day joke that it was proposed to build a perfectly safe road for walkers and horses to the top of the Jungfrau, complete with a toboggan run down on to the Aletsch Glacier. Three years later came the announcement that one of the Eiffel Tower's engineers had worked out plans for a railway to the summit. This was to start with a cog-wheel section, followed by five cable-railway sectors leading to the top. This proved to be no April-foolery. The Jungfrau Railway of today, which took sixteen years (1896–1912) to build, only goes, it is true, as far as Jungfraujoch; from there it is still a three hours' climb to the summit.

The first ascent of the Gross Venediger (12,010 ft) took place on 3 September 1841. Two years later one of the participants, Ignaz von Kürsinger, Imperial Steward at Mittersill in the Upper Pinzgau, published a book about it. The illustration opposite is a detail from its frontispiece. Forty people took part in the climb, though only 26 of them reached the top. The names and occupations of all the participants are known: a milker from the Hoferalp, a farm-hand from the Sulzau, an itinerant vendor, a schoolmaster from Wald, a Doctor of Law from Vienna, a master chimney-sweep from Mittersill—in all a very varied company!

They had responded to an appeal by Kürsinger in the *Salzburger Zeitung*, inviting friends of nature to take part in the attempt to scale the unclimbed peak. 'Explorations into the possibilities of an ascent had preceded the appeal.'

The reality, however, was far removed from the flattering picture's glorification. In his own account Kürsinger reported: 'The strongest party of our whole company pressed on as a vanguard with its guide and the banner, in an effort to reach the summit before the snow should break completely; behind it, the second party toiled more slowly upwards, while the third, still farther below, moved forwards with the greatest difficulty in face of the continual obstacles. By now the vanguard was climbing at a steep angle up the icy snowfield separating the Gross and Klein Venediger, the second party more slowly behind it, while the long line of the bottom-most party became gradually more visible, so that, looking down from above, we could clearly see how one and then another threw himself down on the snow, his strength utterly exhausted, forced to forgo his hope so near to its aim. Gradually shortness of breath, sickness, vomiting, snow-blindness, heart-clutching fear, frozen toes, utter exhaustion and an uncontrollable, almost insatiable thirst laid our rearguard—among which were, unfortunately, the porter carrying the victuals and our trumpeter, charged with the twin duties of blowing the alarm in case of accident and accompanying our summit-toast in case of success—low in the snow. Looking down, we had the impression of a wintry battlefield on which from time to time one of our comrades in the fight was brought down. For here, in the rearguard, the heaviest bodies came to grief first, weary to death of sinking most deeply into the snow; next came those with weak chests; while the skinnier ones, though they looked weaker, if their lungs were still sound, were in fit condition to persevere in the struggle against the indescribable hardships.

'The vanguard and the middle party, among whom was numbered the writer of this essay, moved silently up the steep slope, fighting against those same hardships, which steadily increased the higher we went. We were painfully affected by the sad sight of our comrades as they were struck down one by one, while the uncommonly rarefied air and the almost black sky, against which the gigantic formations of dazzling snow stood out starkly, reminded us that we were drawing nearer to Heaven. Our whole being was seized by a fearful excitement, the like of which we had never experienced; we felt transformed into different creatures, held upright, as we uttered no single word to break the uncanny silence, by the waning hope of reaching our summit. But our ranks, too, now fell prey to distress; and the vanguard bequeathed to us, and we in turn to those of the rearguard who had given in, our own victims to exhaustion; who with corpse-like faces, rendered more ghastly by the black streaks of powder besmirching them, went swaying and staggering down towards their comrades below like drunken men, slowly and with longing looks to the far valley and with many a halt to slumber in the snow.'

After the ascent, the Gross Venediger was for a long time the daily topic of talk in the Pinzgau. 'Much ridiculous bombast got mixed up with it, and in the end reached such a pitch that in Mittersill mine host Rupp's daily guests could only be saved from the ever-recurring topic by the imposition of a fine for every mention of the name Venediger.'

AUS OESTERREICH LEBE HOCH.

'Fog-bows, or phantoms' are one of the most fascinating manifestations of the mountain scene. Whymper saw one after his friends had fallen to their death on the Matterhorn: 'When, lo! a mighty arch appeared, rising over the Lyskamm, high into the sky. Pale, colourless, and noiseless, but perfectly sharp and defined except where it was lost in the clouds, this unearthly apparition seemed like a vision from another world; and, almost appalled, we watched with amazement the gradual development of two vast crosses on either side. It was a fearful and a wonderful sight; unique in my experience and impressive beyond description, coming at such a moment' (above left). Such fog-bows often show the climber himself outlined in the sky ('Spectre of the Brocken'); if he raises his arms the man in thin air does likewise. Fog-bows frequently take fantastic shapes, like the one observed in the Mont Blanc group in 1882 (above right). When the fog thins and suddenly lifts to reveal a peak, the spectacle is always superb, especially when the mountain is as unique as the 984-ft high rock pillar of the Guglia di Brenta (opposite).

All climbers, even today's 'extremists', have reached their level of proficiency on the shoulders of their predecessors. Plate 38 was taken on the entry-pitch to the ice-fields of the Matterhorn's north face.

Plate 39, a lithograph by G. Engelmann, shows an 'ice-walker' in about 1825. To be counted among the classical items of the pictorial documentation of early days of mountaineering are the frontispiece to F. J. Hugi's *Naturhistorische Alpenreise*, which was published in 1830 (Plate 40), and Martin Disteli's *Traverse of the Rottal Glacier* (Plate 41). Disteli had accompanied Hugi on his 'alpine journeys' and both pictures are valuable reflections of technique and equipment at the time. Hugi's purpose was nothing less than to climb the Finsteraarhorn itself, and he indeed reached a point not far from the summit, where they encountered steep ice: 'The very first steps unnerved everyone, and nobody wanted to risk them. Leuthold declared categorically that if I slipped just in front of him, or the hard ice with great bubbles in it broke away, he could not raise a finger to save me. I was too weak to drive my boots firmly into the ice-crust. Attempts to get a grip in stockinged feet seemed even less successful, mainly because my bad foot had become almost frozen while I sat for nearly two hours during the long process of hacking out the steps. The rope did not seem to help at all. Finally Leuthold hung the seven-foot-long stake, thick as an arm, on his back, placed his foot in the first step, allowing it to freeze into it for a moment, then using both hands he drove his pointed stick into the wall, gripped it two-handed for support, and took a second step...'

Such was ice-technique a hundred and fifty years ago.

◂ 38

39

40

41

Mountaineering in the past is depicted on these two pages.

The Emperor Maximilian survived a perilous moment when, in spite of his climbing-irons, he slipped on the steep slabs of a face (Plate 45 is a detail from Leonhard Beck's woodcut for the epic poem 'Theuerdank', published in 1517). In an aquatint of about 1830 (Plate 42) climbers are shown without climbing-irons (crampons) on ice. In those days big shoulder-baskets were carried in place of rucksacks and Plate 46 shows an ascent of the Jungfrau in 1859, using ladders and cutting steps with a woodman's axe. The hunters of the Middle Ages employed a dangerous method of progress-jumping on long poles, as shown in Plate 43. This picture is a detail from a sketch by a Tyrolean master at the end of the 15th century. It is particularly interesting because it is also probably the first representation of roping-down rock ('Abseiling') in existence, to the left of the picture. Plate 44 shows how primitively the rope was handled even in the middle of the last century. In this reconstruction of a rescue on the Great St Bernard Pass, the flimsy sling being lowered to the fallen men is worthy of notice.

43

◄ 42

44

45

46

The face of the climber, then and now. Plate 47 shows unidentified climbers in the western Alps in the mid-19th century. The guide carried the rope – and what a rope! – tied loosely round his hand.

48: Emilio Comici, who made the first ascent of the Grosse Zinne's north face. The picture was taken two months before he fell and was killed in 1940.

49: Konrad Gessner, a pioneer climber during the Renaissance, wrote in 1541 that in future he intended to climb a mountain every year.

50: Leslie Stephen, who made the first ascent of the Schreckhorn in 1861 and wrote the famous *Playground of Europe*.

51: The brothers Franz and Toni Schmid, the first to scale the north face of the Matterhorn in 1931.

52: Jean-Joseph Maquignaz, the fabulous guide who was the first to climb the Dent du Géant and traverse Mont Blanc in winter, then in 1890 failed to return from an ascent of Mont Blanc.

53: Horace-Bénédict de Saussure, the instigator of the first ascent of Mont Blanc in 1786, who himself reached the summit in the following year and by his achievement inspired the ascent of other alpine peaks.

54: Hans Dülfer, who on his first ascent of the Fleischbank east face in 1912 was the first ever to use pitons and a traversing-rope as climbing aids.

55: E. Charlet-Straton, a benevolent middle-aged man, mastered the fearsome Petit Dru in 1897.

56: John Harlin, an addict of modern 'extreme' climbing. In 1966 he fell to his death during the first winter ascent of the 'Direttissima' on the north face of the Eiger.

57: Emil Zsigmondy, the pioneer of guideless climbing, who in 1885 fell to his death from the south-west face of the Meije.

58: Walter Bonatti, whose first solo ascent of the south-west Pillar of the Dru in 1955 made him a legendary figure even in his lifetime.

48

49

◂ 47

50

51

52

53

54

55

56

57

58

Women in the mountains. When in 1838 Henriette d'Angeville climbed Mont Blanc, she wore ankle-length trousers and over them a dress down to her calves (Plate 60). Even on a mountain a lady had to remain feminine. It was not till the last years of the 19th century that some lady-climbers dared to be seen in trousers (Plate 62). As late as 1893 Dent, in his climbing-manual, explained how the long dress – '2¾ yards around the hem should give width enough' – should be caught up while climbing: 'a belt of strong tape should be worn over the dress, which should be firmly attached to it. In this way it can be raised to a greater or less degree, as required. It is quite enough for a safety-pin to secure either side, another the back...' That was how the poor dears were expected to climb! The only reason why Felicitas Carrel, the 'Bride of the Matterhorn', failed to be the first woman to reach the summit was that her long dress hampered her while climbing. All the same she got up to 14,100 ft, to a col which has ever since been called the Col Felicité.

Long dresses were worn for a long time even when ski-ing (Plate 63 dates from 1910). Women were not popular in the mountains till quite recently. In the eyes of many of the men, their place was at the fireside. The Swiss Womens' Alpine Club was only brought into being because the Swiss Alpine Club refused to accept women members. Women had to fight hard for their emancipation in the hills. The girl who climbs so freely today has no conception what a bitter struggle her alpine grandmother had to wage.

Plate 61 shows Daisy Voog, who made her home in Munich, climbing on the north face of the Eiger. In 1964 she became the first woman to defeat the face.

62

60

◀ 59

61

63

Our mountaineering forebears were knights *sans peur et sans reproche!* Today's climbers shudder at their technique. Take, for example, Plate 64, a scene in the Bernese Oberland in 1894; or 67, depicting the second ascent of the Biancograt on Piz Bernina by Karl Schulz with the great Alexander Burgener and Clemens Perren in 1893 (a watercolour by Karl Heubner from one of Schulz's sketches). In both the rope is held in the hand as if it were a posy! In his book, *Mountaineering* (1892), the British climber Dent wrote: 'A rope 20 yards long is quite sufficient for three and, on easy rock, even for four.' Plate 65, entitled 'Protection', is taken from the book in question. Actually, the fallen climber would long ago have dragged the man behind him out of his steps. In those days far too many people went on far too short a rope.

64

Plate 66 illustrates an episode during Whymper's traverse of the Col de Pilatte in the Dauphiné. There was a bergschrund to be crossed. 'Oh! what a *diable* of a place!' cried Reynaud, Whymper's French companion. 'Jump,' cried the others, 'jump'. And then: 'we saw Reynaud, a flying body, coming down as if taking a header into water; with arms and legs all abroad, his leg of mutton flying in the air, his bâton escaped from his grasp; and then we heard a thud as if a bundle of carpets had been pitched out of a window. When we set him upon his feet he was a sorry spectacle: his head was a great snowball; brandy was trickling out of one side of his knapsack, chartreuse out of the other.'

65

66

67 ▸

Mont Blanc, the great adventure. Plate 68 is a photograph taken by Jürgen Winkler in a blizzard on the summit. While the party is fitted out with modern equipment, the blizzards have the same quality as a century ago, when climbers were already active on the mountain, but, as shown in Plate 71, far less well equipped. This is an enlarged detail from a decorative picture, one of the basic documents received by all successful climbers of the mountain in those days. It is questionable whether these collapsing, close-hauled and assiduously-supported figures of misery provided others with a desire to repeat their experiences.

68

Men 'at grips with the mountain' can nonetheless be seen in the lithographs published by a British climber, J. D. Browne, after his ascent in 1853 (Plates 69 and 70). When we look at such pictures we are reminded of one enduring fact: that even nowadays an ascent of Mont Blanc is an exciting experience.

69

70

71 ▸

72

73

The long siege of the Matterhorn ended on 14 July 1865, when men first stood on the sharp summit. The successful climb was made up the Swiss Ridge, the start of which, with the Hörnli Hut, is shown in Plate 74. On the way down four of the triumphant party fell to their death. Gustave Doré depicted the disaster in his famous lithograph (Plate 73).

The first attempt to climb the peak was made in 1857 from its Italian side. Further attempts followed year by year. In 1861 Antoine Carrel (Plate 76) cut his initials in the rock with an ice-axe at the highest point yet reached (Plate 72). A year later Edward Whymper (Plate 78) and his hunch-backed porter Luc Meynet added theirs at the same spot. Whymper and Carrel often joined forces in the battle with the peak, but finished up as competitors. When Whymper at last got to the top, Carrel leading an Italian party up the southern face was only some 600 ft below.

The centenary of the climb was celebrated by the Swiss at Zermatt on 14 July 1965, the programme being subsequently continued on the Italian side at Breuil, where the Matterhorn was illuminated by military searchlights (Plate 77).

74 ▼

▲ 75

◂ 77

76

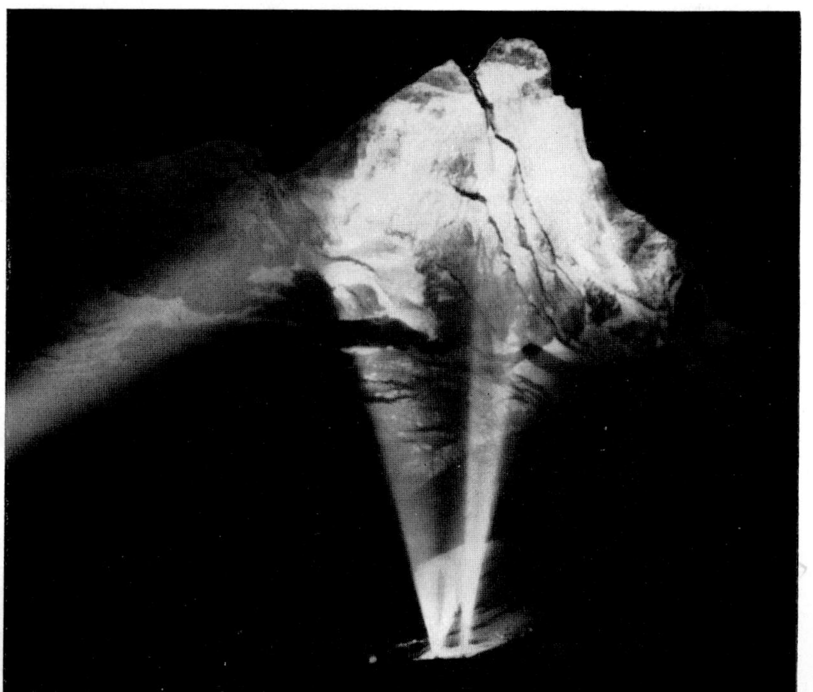

78

Early climbers on virgin rock used to climb in nailed boots, thick clothing and on far too short spacing on the rope. Plate 79 was taken in 1890. Plate 81 is from Dent's 1892 instructional climbing manual. As shown in Plate 80, a photograph taken by Miss Bristow and published in the *Alpine Journal*, A. F. Mummery, the first man to climb the Grépon, tackled the Crack, which has ever since borne his name, in a white shirt and with the rope simply looped around his waist. Even Fritz Kasparek's clothing and equipment on the first climb of the Eiger's north face would be considered harebrained today (Plate 82). Twenty years from now, climbers will again be saying of the present generation: 'Good heavens! Is *that* how poeple climbed then!' Plate 83 shows Herbert Raditschnig on the west face of the Dru; Plate 85 Gaston Rébuffat on the south face of the Aiguille du Midi.

After a French party had climbed Annapurna, the first 'Eight Thousander' (the 14 known peaks in the world of 8000 metres – 26,250 ft – or over), mountaineering became a national sport in France. In 1963, to demonstrate to Parisians how their national heroes mastered the overhangs of Mont Blanc's granite neighbours, a wooden climbing-tower, 70 ft high, was erected on the display-ground of the Union Nationale des Centres de Montagne, with pitons already fixed in place and wooden handholds provided in advance. Plate 84 shows the ascent of the route up the 'roofs'.

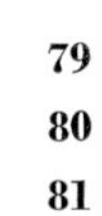

79
80
81

82
83
84

85 ▸

Limestone climbing. Plate 86 shows Michl Innerkofler (1848 to 1888), the first man to climb the Kleine Zinne; he is seen climbing in long trousers. Plate 87 is a drawing by Demeter Diamantidis of the first ascent of the Sasso di Mur in the Dolomites in 1881. The artist's caption says: 'Had Cesaletti slipped at this point, we should not have been able to check even the later stages of his fall.' Today's techniques of rope-management and belaying methods have taken a long time to develop. At that time the best way Casaletti could think of mastering that difficult pitch was to take his boots off. Plate 88 shows Sepp Brunhuber on the south-east face of the Fleischbank in the Kaisergebirge in 1940. Note the soft, pliable Manchon-felt soles, then considered the best. Nowadays no climber would trust himself on rock in such climbing-boots; the life of a Manchon sole was only two or three 1,500-ft climbs. Plate 89 is of Albino Michielli (killed in 1964) on the direct route up the Western Zinne's north face. In 1959 the plastic helmet to protect the climber against falling stones had not yet become standard equipment. The continual improvement in alpine technique and equipment has been a decisive factor in the raising of standards of rock-climbing achievement.

In 1906 the time was not yet ripe for a straightforward ascent of the fearsome Guglia Edmondo de Amicis near Cortina. So Tito Piaz and Bernhard Trier threw a rope over the tip of the sharp needle from the neighbouring Punta Misurina and went across hand over hand on it. Plate 90 was taken on a later repetition of their manœuvre.

86 87

88 89

90 ▶

'Extreme' rock. The north face of the Western Zinne was climbed for the first time in 1935. The Cassin route is still counted as one of the severest climbs in the Dolomites. If the pioneers had been told that the face would one day be climbed *direct* up those terrible yellow precipices they would have dismissed the idea as sheer fantasy. Yet in 1959 two direct routes up the face were opened up: the 'Swiss route' with 310 pitons and 6 expansion-bolts, and the 'French', which demanded 350 and 15 respectively.

How can the kind of climbing shown here give anyone pleasure? Only a man familiar with 'extreme' rock can answer that question. There are those who can really enjoy the limit of exposure. The aspect of the vertical or overhanging rock all around gives the sensation of moving in some mysterious world of its own. The sound as each snap-link snaps into its piton is music to the ear. Especially if the piton holds firm! But there is also a special thrill in moving up on a rickety one. A last-century climber, Eugen Guido Lammer, invented the word 'Nerven-pfeffer' (nerve-spice), a most suitable appellation, for that kind of thrill.

91 92

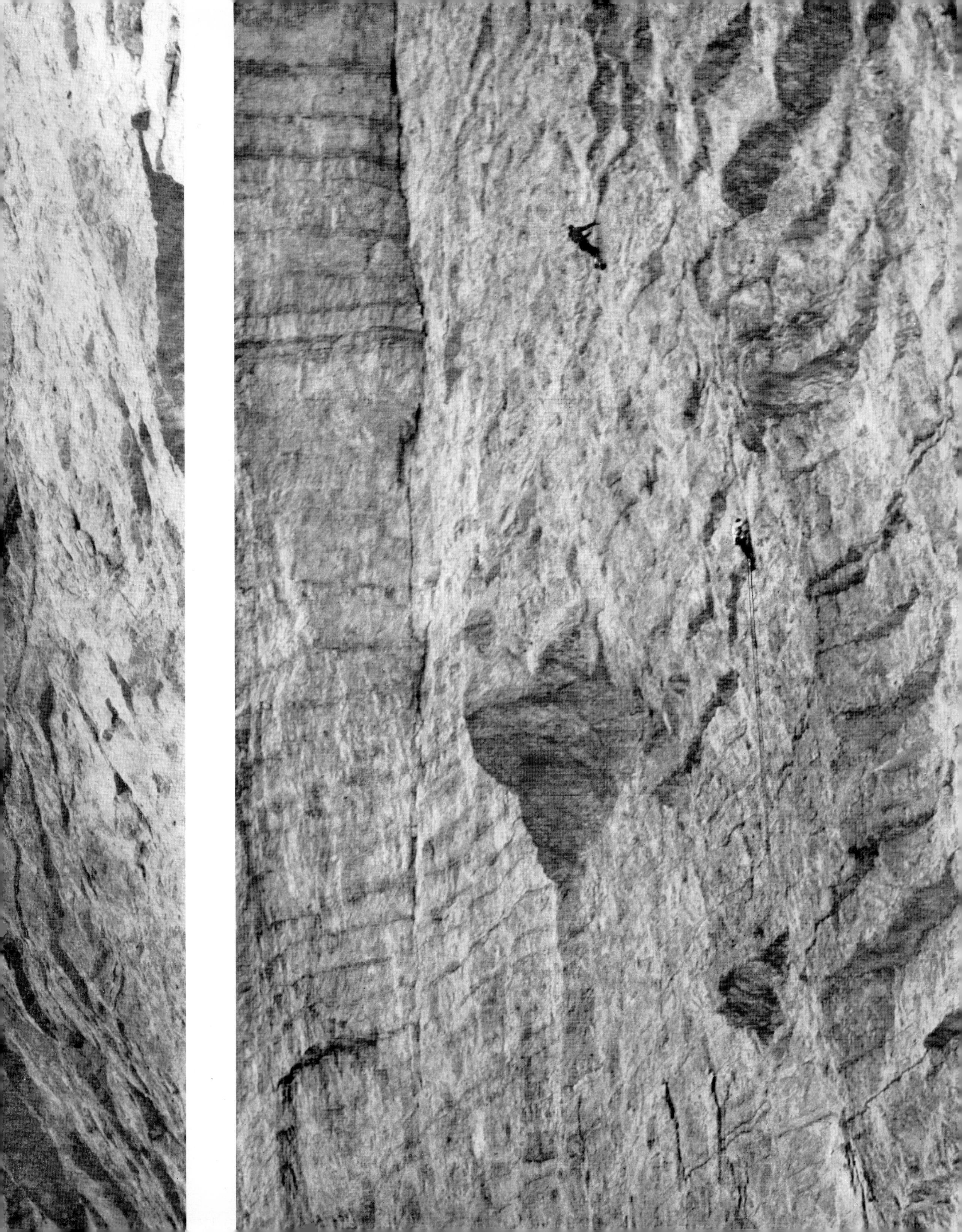

Mountain storms. On his sixth attempt to climb the Matterhorn, Edward Whymper was caught in a thunderstorm. He bivouacked, but got little sleep because the thunder was too noisy. However, 'I forgave the thunder for the sake of the lightning. A more splendid spectacle than its illumination of the Matterhorn crags I do not expect to see.' Recollections of that night in the open were responsible for one of the most striking alpine drawings ever made: Whymper's 'The crags of the Matterhorn during the storm, midnight 10 August 1863' (Plate 93).

A storm blowing up over Piz Bernina's Biancograt provided the photographer Wolf Jürgen Winkler with a splendid picture (Plate 94). All the same, thunderstorms on the high peaks are more than an aesthetic experience; they constitute a danger, indeed the greatest of all alpine perils. Mountaineers in the classical days were never slow to relate the following story to novices: Dr Carl Diener built a 6-ft high cairn on the summit of the Pflerscher Tribulaun. When, only a week later, other climbers got there, they found not a single trace of it. Lightning had annihilated it!

93 94

Nights out in the mountains. In September 1843 Prof. Friedrich Simony, who first explored the Dachstein Group, spent two nights on the summit, the first alone, the second with friends. With stiff fingers Simony did a sketch of himself up there (Plate 98). His bivouac equipment consisted of his coat and a woollen blanket; and there was a fierce blizzard during the night!

During his 'Siege of the Matterhorn' Whymper was already taking a tent along. One of his drawings (Plate 95) shows his camp on the Col du Lion. A gale came up in the night, treatening to blow the tent away; so they struck it and sat on it. Tents in those days were very narrow. Plate 96, from *Pioneers of the Alps*, London 1887, reveals how small a four-man tent was then. Dent wrote: 'Life in a tent demands a great deal of patience. The closer you pack two friends together, the more likely they are to quarrel at times.'

In the winter of 1966, when the 'Direttissima' on the Eiger's north face was climbed in thirty-one days, they took shovels along in order to dig out the kind of bivouac cave in which Dougal Haston, one of the members of the successful climbing-party, is shown in Plate 97.

95

96

97

98

'Salon' mountaineers. The start of the last century saw the awakening of interest in the Alps and by its middle years the so-called 'Swiss Tour' had become fashionable. The blandishments of guides or their own desire to shine prompted many of these pleasure-bound tourists to seek high places – often far too high for their capacities. (Plate 101, from the periodical *Land und Meer*, is not a caricature, though today it looks like one.) At that time numerous albums appeared (the precursors of the modern 'illustrateds') designed to stimulate pleasurable anticipation before one of these 'Swiss Tours' or to revive and retain memories after it. The pictures still appeal to us for their romantic undertones. They show rock-paths and ladder-ways, sampled by people who had found the mountain-life both wonderful and frightening. Plates 99 and 100 are both from the hand of Eugène Querard, who embarked on 'Swiss Tours' in mid-century, to collect pictorial subjects – a forerunner of today's press photographers.

99 100

101 ▸

L. Bechstein

Mountain accidents. In 1887 six young Swiss set out to climb the Jungfrau. Caught in a blizzard, they fell and were all killed. Plate 103 is included as a reminder to all climbers that the line between triumph and disaster in mountaineering is slender indeed.

Mountain accidents led to the foundation of rescue services. The first of such organizations was formed in Vienna in 1898: a Rescue Section, brought into being at the instigation of the Alpine Clubs. Volunteers undertook not to leave the city over the week-end, so as to be ready to respond immediately to an emergency call. The chief problem in those days was how to get the rescue teams to the scene of the accident quickly enough, in view of the limited transport facilities available. Plate 104 shows the primitive methods then in use to bring the injured down from the mountains. Today the only unsolved problem facing the alpine rescue services is how to get people overwhelmed by avalanches out in time. Avalanche-dogs have their uses, but considerable limitations. Many experts refuse to accept the latest avalanche search-equipment – the Förster-Sonde and the Stöx Magnetic Signal – as sufficiently developed. Fierce arguments arose between supporters of the dogs and the 'probes' (see Plates 105 and 106). In ten years these heated debates will have been forgotten, but they will have resulted in even swifter aid to the victims of mountaineering accidents.

102

103

105

Tafel XXXXI
Fig. 139
Fig. 141
Fig. 142
Dr Oskar Bernhard, Samaden
Samariterdienst
Verlag von Simon Tanner, Samaden
J. J. Sigg, Winterthur
420.009
BERN

104

106

Summits. Every climber wants to get to the top. In bygone days climbers loved to take flags up with them, just as today pennants are still carried to Himalayan heights. Later, crosses were erected on the tops (Plate 107). Plate 108 shows the summit-shelter on Triglav.

There is neither cross nor cairn on the highest mountain in the Alps, Mont Blanc, though once a complete house stood there. As long ago as 1891 a Swiss engineer, Infeld, at the instigation of the French scientist Janssen, had driven a 164-ft tunnel into the ice-cap of the summit-structure. The idea was to bore through the ice to solid rock and, having exposed it, to build an observatory on it. But when no rock was encountered, it was decided to build it on the ice. Güssfeldt, watching the building operations after his first traverse of the Peuterey Ridge in 1893, was highly critical. 'If my theories of the movement of ice on high mountains are correct', he maintained, 'the observatory is bound to sink gradually, rather like an object supported by a pack of cards when one card after another is withdrawn from under it. It is an open question how quickly the sinking process will proceed. If it takes place so slowly that there is plenty of time to record the observations as intended, the observatory will have justified itself completely.

109

110

After all, the activities of a human being are confined within a limited life-time.' Plate 109 shows the house on Mont Blanc and the man who built it. It stood there for seventeen years.

◂ 107

108

People whom circumstances debar from climbing mountains are often powerfully affected by the longing to reach high summits. There was a blind Englishman who insisted on being led to the top of the Matterhorn; and Plate 110 shows a crippled Englishwoman who, in about 1890, had herself carried on a stretcher to the summit of Nuvolau by guides from Cortina.

Inside the mountains. The pot-holer enjoys his thrills in silence and in darkness. Plate 111 is a watercolour by Engineer Hermann Bock, portraying the first penetration by man into the Tristan Dome of the Giant Ice-cave on the Dachstein. After the descent of a 98-ft wire-rope ladder, the ice was reached. 'The explorers watched the work of the leader, as he cut steps, as if from a gigantic theatre-box. At first it was possible to safeguard him on a diagonal rope, but later he had to force a way into the pitch darkness of the mountain-ice with hefty swings of his axe, totally unprotected. The light of the cave-lamp crept higher and higher up the wall beyond, step by hazardous step, till a great sigh of relief greeted the plucky climber as he reached the high ice-chamber.'

▲ 111

◄ 112

The Geldloch on the Ötscher was first explored at about the turn of the century and the photograph of the 'spectres of the cave' (Plate 112, from the Journal of the German and Austrian Alpine Club) was taken at the time, in 1902. 'A stone trickling slowly down a débris-chute in the background awoke a sound like that of someone climbing down it; by chance our lanterns, pointing in that direction, produced a trick of lighting, which quite plainly seemed to reveal a white figure bending forwards and looking at us.' The figure was a rock, and the experience inspired the spoof-photograph, in which the 'spectres of the Ötscher' were captured 'with the aid of two friends who dressed up for the part and the well-known trick of ghost-photography.' (Eugen Beer).

Plate 114 depicts the 'harp' in the Tennengebirge's Sulzer-Ofen; and 113, the first bivouac-box ever erected in a pot-hole. It is situated in the Tantal Cave (Hagengebirge) 3,300 ft below the surface and a whole day's journey from the entrance.

113

▼ 114

Non-north-face climbing. Plate 116 is a photograph taken on Meran's fashionable Gilfpromenade, where in 1901 'a photographer Fritz Lagarjoli had set up a "transportable" studio for postcard snapshots. Snowshoes, crampons, ropes, etc. are there. The "beetling crag" is in stock, too; so anybody who wants to be photographed for the benefit of his "no-head-for-heights" friends and relations in the most hair-raising situation will find all he needs for a few shillings. The "climb" will take place only a foot or two from the beautifully maintained Gilfpromenade' (from the *Deutsche Alpenzeitung*, 1901).

The 'Alpine Club enjoying itself on the Jungfrau' (Plate 118) is a drawing of Karl Reinhardt's in 1869; the caricature of climbers having themselves carried to a summit (Plate 115) is dated 1882. The great success of Hubert Mumelter's *Bergfibel* ('The Mountain Primer'), published in 1934, from which Plate 117 reproduces a page, proves that mountaineers do not only care for north faces. Toni Hiebeler calls Plate 120 'Grade-Sex climbing'; and Plate 119 shows the 'Narrenschrift' (addicts' signatures) on the Wank, near Garmisch Partenkirchen.

If, on a traverse you should chance
To lose your balance, hold or stance,
You will most painfully become,
Spite all belays, a pendulum.
Which, on a thousand-metre face,
Suspended airily in space,
Is an entirely different thing
From jiggling on a leading-string.

OVERLEAF: The full-page photograph shows Grade VI climbing in the Mont Blanc group. The climbers on the east face of the Grand Capucin are ringed by the white circle.

115

116

117

118 119 ▼ 120 ▶

STUTTGART
HÜLS
PULHEIM
BERLIN
HELM
KÖLN
MEMMINGEN
LEIBERSDORF
SOLINGEN
ESSEN
WUPPERTAL
WEIDEN
BAD OEYNHAUSEN
CELLE
RIETBERG
KASSEL
ARNSBERG
KA
PARIS

Fritz Kasparek's account of his (the fourth) ascent of the north face of the Western Zinne by the Cassin route in 1937 horrified thousands of those who heard him lecture or read his book, and they said so.

'It took a long time to get the piton in. It wouldn't go more than about half an inch into the rock. I looked at it with deep distrust and tried to bang one in higher up. The same story. The next few pitons went in about the same distance and wobbled disturbingly when the weight of a foot-sling came on them. Whenever I called down to my second to haul on the rope, I added: "but gently, or the thing'll come out!" After gaining some twenty feet in this precarious fashion, I could find no place for a piton to get me up any further.

'I worked away for two hours, without the slightest result. Every time I tried to move up, I felt I was on the verge of falling and had to go back. Down at the bottom I could see Friedl and Anni, who had come for our boots. Later on, they told us that they had never seen anything so terrifying as the sight of that yellow wall, on whose most overhanging part the two of us were stuck.

'I myself was utterly amazed when, after three hours, I had not gained a single inch. Every time I considered taking a chance, I was brought to my senses by the suspicious wobbling of my last piton and a glance downwards. Had I fallen, I should have landed on the scree slopes sixty feet out from the base of the wall, so overhanging was the face. It was only after suggesting a retreat, and deciding on it after one last attempt, that I discovered a minute fissure behind a flake. I managed to drive a piton in nearly half an inch, inserted a sling and called for a pull on the rope. Tensed for a fall, I held my breath as I watched the piton. There was a loud "ping" as the lower one, on which I had hung for three hours, came out. I didn't care any more. Three feet further up, I got another one in and I had hardly called for a pull up on the rope when the one below came out too. This nerve-racking manœuvre, with the height of a possible fall increasing all the time, had to be twice repeated before I reached safety at the lateral band above.'

'How many men are there who can survive such an ordeal?' was the question on everyone's lips at the time. Fritz Kasparek who, in the following year, was a member of the first party to climb the north face of the Eiger, was one of the finest climbers of the 'thirties. Everybody was asking whether such performances marked the peak of alpine possibilities. Yet, today, the Cassin route on the Zinne is just 'the old route'. Direct routes, still more severe, have been opened up on that wall, and these have even been climbed solo! Have climbers, then, become even more skilful?

When Kasparek did his climb, he wore no protection on his head. He wore a short 'windcheater' blouse reaching to his hips (which was then fashionable) and wide plus-four trousers halfway down his calves (also the fashion at the time). The ropes were heavy hemp ones, requiring hard work to manipulate when they ran through several pitons. The pitons were steel (and therefore equally heavy) and so were the snap-links or 'Karabiner'. His climbing-boots had undressed-leather uppers and a felt sole (the famous Manchon soles). They were soles which only gripped properly when slightly damp, a state often produced on severe pitches by methods not exactly suited to the drawing-room.

Is it, then, the equipment which has improved?

The truth is that *everything* has improved, the climber himself and his equipment. The passage of time has changed so much: the climber's relationship to his mountain, climbing-techniques, equipment, the lot! After all, everything in this world is dictated by Time—even the 'Conquest of the Useless', as that great French climber Lionel Terray called mountaineering.

THE DEVELOPMENT OF SKIING

Erwin Mehl

'It could be argued whether there is any activity demanding greater pluck and skill. There is no gainsaying that it will take you into a world more beautiful and more out of the ordinary than any other pursuit.'—Henry Hoek.

The view expressed in these two sentences by that sensitive writer and one-time ski-champion of Germany has, within the span of a man's life, stimulated the greatest impetus developed by any single bodily exercise in the private, communal or economic life of our times.

No other exercise—gymnastics excepted—has held in thrall so many men and women, experts and moderate performers alike, from the days of their youth to their old age, calling them in rapidly growing numbers year by year up into the 'hills, from whence'—in the words of the Psalmist—'cometh our help'. And the great appeal to mountain-lovers is just that the joy of skiing is simply the joy of the hills, enhanced by the joy of the downhill run.

It is surprising that it took so long to discover this marvellous source of health and human delight: in Austria and Germany not till 1891, in Scandinavia thirty years earlier, though there are clear indications that the equipment existed there from the Stone Age onwards, that is, a matter of some 5,000 years. Its revival stems from the mode of life and surroundings of human beings. It was not till their concentration in cities, barring men from nature and natural movement, had reached a sufficient pitch that there sprang up a growing desire for exercise and life in natural surroundings.

The year 1860 was a turning-point for every kind of bodily exercise in Europe—gymnastics, swimming, skating and various English forms of sport. In the northern lands this new urge lifted skiing from an amusement among the peasants to the level of a national sport: in Central Europe it took another thirty years to popularize this winter-sport, although its existence was known from books or isolated personal experience.

Right at the outset of snow-running in Central Europe there is an account by the Governor of Carniola, Weichard Freiherr von Valvasor, which is as valuable for its contents as for the medieval language in which they are expressed. In the first of the four volumes constituting his *Die Ehre des Herzogtums Krain* ('The Glory of the Earldom of Carniola', Laibach 1689, reprinted 1877), he describes a 'rare invention' of the Slovene peasants, especially in the region of Auersperg, by which 'they do in winter-time, when lies the snow, run down from the top of some high hill with unbelievable speed.

'They take wooden boards twain, to a quarter-Zoll [¼ in] thick, broad the half of a working-boot [6 in] and of the length of about five such boots [5 ft]. At front, such little boards are bent and curled upwards; and in their midst stands a strap of leather wherein to place the feet. Of these boards a man hath on either foot one. Thereto doth the peasant take in hand a strong stick, which he placeth under his armpit, leaning thereon strongly backwards, so steering and pushing himself down over the steepest of hills. Whereby I can best describe, he shooteth or flieth downwards. For insomuch as he standeth on his small boards and leaneth with might and main on his stick, slideth he so swiftly downwards as to surpass all credence and yieldeth not a whit to those in Holland who run upon the ice on stride-shoes [the old word for skates] in speed.'

For many years it was thought that this accomplishment had long since lapsed, till in 1930 more intense research on the plateau of Bloke, to the south of Laibach, revealed the astonishing fact that the snow-running of the peasants described by Valvasor was still in use there, in exactly the same manner as in the Governor's days. Unfortunately, the Second World War put an end to this unique revelation of cultural history, for in 1942 the Italian Occupation Authorities demanded the handing-in of all skis, including the ancient ones, so as to deprive the Resistance of their use. The peasants, however, preferred to make a bonfire of them, so very few pairs survived the war.

We are indebted to the Director of the Ethnographic Museum at Laibach (Ljubljana), Boris Orel, for making available to other museums pictorial representations of the original skis preserved there, and publishing in 1956 and 1965 two excellent pamphlets about them; thus establishing that these 'Boardlets' were brought with them by the Slovenes who migrated to Carniola in about AD 600 from their northern homes, and have survived as a unique instance of deplacement for more than a thousand years.

As long ago as 1795 one of three classical gymnasts (GutsMuths, Vieth and Jahn), following the guidance of a Norwegian at the Philanthropinum in the Schnepfenthal near Gotha, fashioned a pair of 'boards' of unequal length, as was the practice till well into the nineteenth century, with a 5- to 6-foot 'pusher' ski for the right foot and another, 7 foot long or a little longer, a 'glider', for the left. On these, through the Forest of Thüringen, he traced the first Central European ski-tracks, if we except Carniola. So thrilled was he with this new form of exercise that he advocated it in the second edition of his famous *Gymnastics for the Young* ('Gymnastik für die Jugend', 1804, pp. 386–90). The title he gave the passage was: 'Snow-running, or running on snow-shoes'.

With it, the expression 'snow-running' (*cf.* 'ice-running') first appeared in print. GutsMuths gives a few details about the development of the equipment, its military usage in the North, then a full description of the equipment, with a sketch from his own hand, and finally an introduction to single-stick running. It reaches its climax in the downhill-run. 'Now the snow-shoes become pinions on which one runs downwards almost without effort, more swiftly or more slowly according to one's judgment of the slope.'

How well the Old Master knew the value of this activity, how enthusiastically did he describe it! But he was far ahead of his time. His chapter was soon forgotten and only brought to light again in 1925.

When the English national movement for outdoor and sporting activities in about 1860 reached Scandinavia, townsmen there began to contemplate snow-running, and first among them the inhabitants of Christiania, as Oslo was then called.

The farmers and woodcutters of Telemark (the District of 'Mark' of Thelir), where the mountains rise to 3,000 feet, taught the men of Christiania downhill-running and jumping on skis, which was already highly developed. But among the low hillocks of Christiania, whose 1,600-foot Tryvanshöhe is the highest point, cross-country skiing supplanted downhill running. Cross-country and jumping—still 'the northern divergence' today—were, however, confined to Fennoskandia till 1891. The outside world failed to master those skills; so, at first, all attempts to popularize them beyond the northern lands failed.

The change came at a single stroke when, in 1891, the German edition of Fridtjof Nansen's *First Crossing of Greenland* appeared. The Norwegian edition in the previous year had not had much success. In his book Nansen reports his gigantic performance: in the autumn of 1888, in the space of forty days, he had traversed Greenland from east to west, a journey of 350 miles across the inland ice, involving an ascent of 9,000 feet from sea-level. He and his companions had travelled on rimless oak boards, 7 feet long, with leather bindings and three grooves in the under-side (as in jumping-skis) while hauling their heavy sleds, loaded with all their equipment. Nansen hymned the delights of skiing loudly. It was natural for such a book to arouse the greatest interest in Central Europe. A host of readers were gripped by what Zdarsky called 'Nansen Fever'.

They sent to Norway for the 'Magic Boards', on the basis 'the longer, the better'—7 feet, 8 feet, 9 feet long, rimless, with leather or tubular-steel bindings. With them they made attempts on meadows, on the city's ice-rinks; they climbed hills, described their experiences in the papers, founded clubs, organized races (those in Mürzzuschlag were the first), published periodicals, wrote little primers . . . and then gave the whole thing up. And small wonder, when one takes into account the unsuitable equipment, the method of running involved (the looseness of the bindings permitted only 'leaning back' turns, like the 'Telemark') and the total lack of amenities for practising the sport.

Alfred Steinitzer of Würzburg, the author of the picture-book *Alpinismus in Bildern* (1913), wrote in 'Reports of the German and Austrian Alpine Club' (1894), in an article about the suitability of the (round) Canadian snow-shoe in high mountains: 'I should like to start by saying that, in my view, for high tours in winter the Canadian snow-shoe is far superior to the ski. Indeed, I would dismiss the latter as utterly unusable on long high-altitude tours.' Yet, during the First World War, Steinitzer was to command a ski-battalion!

The well-known Stuttgart writer on mountaineering, Theodor Wundt, too, stated in an 1895 article about 'Equipment for winter tours', with regard to the 'Boards': 'Going uphill is extremely tiring and difficult, running downhill very dangerous. It is almost impossible to avoid obstacles and once you fall, which you are highly likely to do, you are positively helpless in this long footgear. However, my strongest objection to them is that on one occasion the august customs officials at Kufstein charged me an incredible duty on them as "luxury leather-goods".'

Nowadays, if you examine those early examples in a museum, you cannot really quarrel with the two views just cited. The Norwegian type of ski was all right for running on the level or in hillocky ground, but not for alpine or sub-alpine slopes of great steepness, nor for the long downhill runs which were beginning to replace cross-country skiing. Equipment, methods, and above all the instruction in their application, as well as accommodation and traffic-routes, needed adaptation to the new requirements. Scandinavian ski-running had to be transformed into alpine skiing. The task was undertaken and fulfilled by the 'pathfinders' of the day up to the outbreak of the First World War. During it the high alpine front-line, running up to the 12,802-foot Ortler, established once and for all the worth of the ski and brought about the unification of skiing technique and instructions.

The Alps were the springboard, and later remained the headquarters, of all future ski-mountaineering. Every important stride forward in its equipment, with the exception of the American metal ski, and in technique and the instructional approach, was first made in the Alps. It was from there and not from Scandinavia that skiing embarked on its world-wide triumph. Alpine instructors are sought all over the globe. It is therefore justifiable to speak of the purely alpine development of skiing.

If one keeps one's eye firmly on the crucial 'inside development', the technical and instructional aspect, the first great chapter in the rise of skiing falls into four subsidiary sections, naturally overlapping to some extent and not distinctly separated from one another, because the new form of the activity for a time continued alongside the old style, running parallel with it. We can, however, subdivide it as follows:

THE NORWEGIAN ERA: this dates from Nansen (1891) to Bilgeri's text-book (1910). Features: tubular fastenings and Huitfeldt binding, 'lean-back' turns (Hollow Cross Christiania and Telemark), the simultaneous practice of running with a single stick or with two, the Central European Clubs (Switzerland 1904, Germany and Austria 1905).

THE LILIENFELD ERA: from Zdarsky's book in 1896 to 1918. The Lilienfeld binding, the first really good one. 'Forward-lean' turns with the single stick, the first coordinated approach to instruction, the first ski text-book, the Alpine Ski Club (1900) and the first Slalom (1905).

THE BILGERI ERA: from Bilgeri's book (1910) to the end of the war in 1918. The Bilgeri binding, alongside Lilienfeld and Huitfeldt bindings, running with two sticks, the introduction of the Stemm-turn, instruction in a drill which broke up the whole motion into its component movements and was practised with preliminary exercises.

THE FIRST WORLD WAR (1914–18): general introduction of skiing on the alpine front, chiefly for communications and supplies. As chief of all ski operations in the Austro-Hungarian army, Bilgeri unified technique and training methods along his own lines.

A few additional 'highlights':

The 'Norwegian' era. Descriptions, which I collected in the Zdarsky *Festschrift* (1936), give some idea of the standards at that time. A section by Zdarsky, entitled 'For Skiers', in the Austrian Ski Club's Journal at the beginning of the 'nineties runs as follows: 'The greatest achievement of the ski-runner is really that he visits high mountains. For the downhill run, the skier crouches at the top of the slope, leans firmly back on his stick and shuts his eyes. Then he tears downhill with the speed of an arrow until his breath fails him. At that point he has to throw himself sideways on to the snow and waits till he gets his breath back; he then resumes his downhill flight, his loss of breath, his rest lying on the snow, and so on till he reaches the bottom.'

One indication of the enthusiasm and applied zeal of the skiers of the day was their ability to accomplish big mountain tours on these totally unsuitable pieces of equipment and, till 1900, without the aid of skins. For example, in 1890 Karl Otto climbed the 6,000-foot Heimgarten near Murnau in the Allgau; on 13 February 1891, two Styrians, Max Kleinoscheg of Graz and Toni Schruf of Mürzzuschlag, and K. Wenderich climbed the slightly higher Stuhleck, the first really big 'ski-summit' in Austria. In 1893 Dr Stäubli of Zürich reached the summit of the Arosa Rothorn, the first 'Near Three Thousander Ski-peak', 9,794 feet high; on 5 February 1894 Wilhelm von Arlt (born 1853 in Prague, moved to Salzburg in 1890 and died 1941) climbed the 10,200-foot Rauriser Sonnblick, the first genuine 'Three Thousander' to be mastered on skis—the descent to Kolm-Saigurn taking 32 minutes, and only 23 on a repetition of the climb on 17 April 1895. On 13 January 1896, W. Paulcke, E. Bauer, V. de Beauclair and P. Sterring made the first three-thousand-metre ascent in the Western Alps when they stood on the summit of the Oberalpstock (10,926 feet); after which, Paulcke and four others, between 18 and 23 January 1897, traversed the whole Bernese Oberland from the Grimsel, across the Oberaarjoch (10,607 feet), Grünhornlücke (10,844 feet) to the 11,300-foot Jungfraujoch, and back to Belalp.

On 30 August 1896 W. von Arlt accomplished the first summer climb on skis when he ascended the Johannisberg (11,375 feet). On 23 March 1898 Oskar Schuster of Munich and the Austrian Heinrich Moser climbed Monte Rosa, the first 'Four Thousander' to be ascended on skis, 15,217 feet high. Between 24 and 26 February 1904, Hugo Mylins of Hanover, with two guides, got as far as the Vallot Refuge (14,000 feet) on Mont Blanc on skis.

These were all magnificent feats by outstandingly gifted performers, fit enough to master the Alps on skis; there was as yet no sign of any alpine skiing in which the majority of

This woodcut, which purports to be the oldest representation of a ski-jump, was in fact an April Fool's Day joke that appeared in the periodical *Winter* in 1923. There was a legend that Styrkar, a Norwegian under sentence, was promised a pardon for his crime if he could jump from a high mountain without hurting himself. Styrkar jumped wearing 'boards' and came to no harm. The artist Toni Schönecker made a drawing to illustrate this attractive story, and it was taken as gospel by many readers who saw it. As late as 1933 the drawing was being published in the United States as 'the oldest picture of a ski-jump', in spite of all intervening efforts to explain the true position.

ordinary men could take an interest. It was Matthias Zdarsky (1856–1940) who prepared the ground for a general sport of skiing with his 'Alpine (Lilienfeld) Ski Technique' in November 1896 (renamed 'The Technique of Alpine Skiing' from the 4th edition in 1908 onwards). Zdarsky was a German Bohemian from the formerly German-speaking enclave of Iglau. Owing to the loss of his left eye he went to school late, but became a teacher, painter and sculptor, finally devoting himself to the husbandry of a property called Habernreit which he had bought from Lilienfeld, where as a bachelor he had also to run the house single-handed. In 1916, when he was sixty and alpine adviser on the First War's Carinthian front, he was crippled for life on a rescue operation in the Gailtal, when a second avalanche struck the rescue party. What an irony of fate, seeing that he was the greatest avalanche expert of his time! At Christmas 1939 increasing pain from his injuries forced him to leave Habernreit, after exactly fifty years of tenancy. He died at St Pölten on 20 June of the following year and was buried on his own land. His wonderful services to skiing are embodied in the *Festschrift*, 200 pages long and containing 100 pictures, which I edited for his eightieth birthday at Vienna in 1936.

Zdarsky was by common consent the greatest skier of his time. As long ago as 1896, on a 22° slope 200 yards long, he reached a speed of 65 m.p.h. He also did a reverse somersault (the 'Auerbach Salto') while running downhill on skis and, on small jumps of his own construction, achieved a distance of nearly 70 feet. To his bodily skill was added an unusually penetrative mind directed to everything he laid a hand to, an extraordinary technical mastery and a quite unusual gift for teaching, in which he delighted.

This all went to make Zdarsky one of the most outstanding and influential personalities in the world of skiing and amongst the founders of the sport. It was he who laid down all its solid bases, among them the first really usable alpine binding, in 1896, which by the provision of an indestructible steel plate provided the two absolute requisites, even to this day—namely a completely firm lateral hold of the ankles and their properly-sprung connection with the board of the ski; in addition, its special feature was the freedom of the ankle to achieve an extreme angle of forward separation from the ski (the binding made it possible to lie flat on one's stomach). This is no longer possible with any of the modern bindings, but at the time it saved innumerable injuries to bones and tendons, resulting from the immobilization of the foot by the lateral bindings during a headlong fall, especially if the body is turned in its course.

Another discovery of Zdarsky's was how to match the length of the ski to the stature of the body (in roughly the same proportions as today) and their breadth to the weight of the performer. This and his single-stick technique enabled Zdarsky to discover the safest and most easily and swiftly imparted method of skiing ever perfected. For it must be openly admitted that no method with two sticks can come anywhere near it. This is proved by the wonderful results Zdarsky obtained as an instructor, as for instance when, after a three-weeks' army course for beginners at Gastein in 1908, according to a 17-folio report in the military archives at Vienna, every single participant safely negotiated slopes of 50°. No matter how excellent, no 'two-stick' instruction could match that result. Nearly every beginners' course today counts its toll of accidents.

Among his achievements were the inventions of the 'Torlauf' (Gate-Course) in 1905, the Zdarsky Tent, still indispensable today, the bases for an avalanche notification service and many other things. This all contributed to his selection for the work of establishing the ski-arm of the Austrian army. From 1903 to 1910 he held numerous instructional courses for the army and laid down the 'Introduction to Military Skiing' for the military in 1908. His work is commemorated by a statue erected at Lilienfeld in 1965.

If safety had been the only consideration in mountain skiing, the Zdarsky single-stick technique would have been sufficient, but the greater freedom of movement when two sticks are used was a new attraction. Georg Bilgeri (1873–1934), an officer in the Kaiserjäger, championed its cause. He was a slim, elegant performer, an enthusiastic climber, very inventive in matters of equipment, and to cap everything, an idealist, who taught some forty thousand pupils without any kind of monetary reward. On 4 December 1934, while demonstrating an exercise on Innsbruck's Patscherkofel, he ruptured his aorta and died all too early.

The removal of the single stick by his new method of instruction—Nansen had called it 'the true support in every emergency'—greatly increased the danger of falling, and so of injury. It has ever since remained the weak point in the 'two-stick' method, as evidenced today by the thousands of casualties brought into hospital on any fine Sunday in winter. Had the single-stick method been retained, only a fraction of this number would have suffered injury. Bilgeri attempted to reduce the danger of a fall by introducing the braking motion of the Stemm-turn, carried out in mid-balance, as the focal point of his method, to replace the Zdarsky turn executed with the balance thrown forward (*Alpine Skiing*, 1910). It was this new turn which Hannes Schneider adopted as the key-point of his teaching at his world-famous Arlberg School.

Bilgeri taught the movements of skiing by breaking them up into their component parts as follows: Running diagonally—putting the weight on the lower ski, pushing off with the upper one—transferring the weight to the upper ski and so facilitating a turn with the body beyond the vertical, advancing ('brushing-past') of the inner ski during the turn—running diagonally. These 'requisites for the proper motion' were shouted at the 'moving pupil'—mostly in vain—and had to be executed intentionally. It was because Bilgeri was entrusted with the whole organization of skiing on the alpine front during the First World War, and because good skiers joined the ski-battalions, that this technique gradually supplanted the single-stick method. It is remarkable that while, from about 1896 onwards till the end of the First World War, a new technique entirely suitable for alpine skiing had been developing, till 1930 competition had remained entirely confined to cross-country racing (the northern 'Langlauf') and to jumping—in itself almost irrelevant to alpine skiing—strong evidence of the unreliability of the bindings then in use. The only exception was—Zdarsky. As long ago as 19 March 1905 he set out the course for the first 'gate-running' competition in the history of skiing on the 4,000-foot Muckenkogel near Lilienfeld, a mile and a half long, with a drop of 1,600 feet and 85 'gates', including 7 'hairpins'. That was seventeen years before the first gated race instituted by Arnold Lunn, the English skier at Mürren in 1922, and then he gave it, erroneously, the Norwegian name of 'Slalom'.[1]

The first known picture of a woman on skis is to be found in a book by the Archbishop of Upsala, Olaus Magnus, *Historia de gentibus septentrionalibus*, published in Rome in 1555. The book deals with the life and customs of those who lived in the Northlands. The caption in the German edition which appeared later runs: 'The womenfolk too do proceed on the hunt, with their hand-bows and letting their hair fly abroad as standeth in the figure pictured here.'

[1] The Slalom practised in Telemark was originally a downhill race on a slope of even angle—the *Slad* (evenly tilted) *lom* (ski-track), in contra-distinction to the *Hoppe-lom*, the jumping-track. Later the men of Telemark did introduce obstacles in the Slalom in direct contradiction of the name, whose meaning they had forgotten. But no Norwegian Slalom ever had flagged gates. Zdarsky had already invented these in 1901. He once said about his having kept this a secret: 'I am the idiot who was the key to the gate.'

Praktische Anleitung
zur
Erlernung des Schneeschuh-
(Ski-)Laufens
für Touristen, Jäger, Forstleute und Militärs.

Mit 33 Illustrationen.
Herausgegeben von Theodor Neumayer, München
Schneeschuhfabrikant und Armeelieferant.

Hamburg 1893.

Verlagsanstalt und Druckerei A.-G. (vormals J. F. Richter).
Königl. Schwedisch-Norwegische Hofdruckerei und Verlagshandlung.

A ski-school in 1893. In the frontispiece to Neumayer's Ski Manual (shown above), a couple are seen gliding down through the winter landscape arm in arm. The lower picture comes from the same instructional handbook, and is the first representation of a 'nursery slope'. Most of the skiers are seen using only one stick, but one man is already using two, as is modern practice.

After the war, skiing took an unparalleled leap forward, mainly, at first, in the Alps. Hundreds of thousands on the alpine fronts had discovered the beauty of the mountains in winter and how it could be unlocked by skiing; they were doubly grateful for such a source of pleasure because times were hard for men recovering from the ravages of war. There were hardly enough resorts and ski-refuges to accommodate the visiting crowds.

The army, the customs, the police were equipped, and the influence of a totally unexpected force became a leading factor in the general development: Dr Arnold Fanck's films, in which slow motion was applied for the first time—*Snow-shoe Marvels* (1925, also the title of his book, the best illustrated skiing book yet to appear), *Engadine Fox-hunt*, *The White Magic*, and *Sun over the Arlberg*. In the first place these films spread the fame of Hannes Schneider, his chief assistant, all over the world; then Schneider set a seal on it with the marvellously organized school he ran at St Anton in the Arlberg. It was not unusual for him to have 2,000 pupils at a time. Those were the days when the Stemm-turn had reached the zenith of its popularity, which was soon to decline gradually. Even Hannes himself had long given up stemming, and was 'swinging' or 'weaving' down the slopes: indeed, by the end of the 'twenties he was insisting on 'weaving' as an item in the tests for ski-instructors.

It was therefore natural for everyone else to want to 'swing' or 'weave', and with justification when, in 1928, the Kandahar races founded by Arnold Lunn and Schneider resulted in a fierce rise in the speed of downhill running and, at the same time, Toni Seelos with his 'parallel swing' discredited the reputation of both Stemm- and Christiania-turns. The methods of instruction simply had to keep pace with these developments.

Dr Friedrich Hoschek of Vienna, at the same time a medical practitioner and gymnastics instructor, who was killed at Stalingrad in 1942, had been a pupil of Dr Karl Gaulhofer, the founder of the natural method of gymnastics-instruction in schools; with his book *The Natural Way to Learn Skiing* he showed the way to the natural method of instruction in the turns.

After a long struggle this new method of teaching turns finally prevailed and was splendidly illustrated by Stefan Kruckenhauser's pictures in the Austrian plan for ski-instruction of 1957. Today the Stemm-turn plays a very minor part; the more up-to-date 'weaving' has won pride of place.

This reversal was greatly assisted by a great improvement in technical aids. After the end of the 'twenties, the rapid increase in the number of ropeways, chair- and drag-lifts increasingly relegated the old soft-snow skiing to the background; or to put it more accurately, the number of those who undertook skiing tours remained stationary (limited by the accommodation the huts could manage to provide), while the number of those who used the ropeways and ski-lifts increased many times over. The *pistes* they used, however, were soon beaten into very hard snow, and therefore suitable for parallel turns and 'weaving'. It frequently happens that because skiers prefer the hard-surfaced runs there is virgin snow alongside them. For this reason, too, instruction was reversed in favour of 'swinging'. In the field of competition, a strange thing happened: the so-called 'Giant Slalom' was revived in exactly the form of Zdarsky's 1905 innovation. Since Lunn's 'Gated Race' was short and cramped, with a multiplicity of gates (40 to 50 in a fall of 500 feet), Dr Gunter Langes of Bozen marked out on the Marmolata's wide glacier-field—exactly 30 years to the day after Zdarsky's race on the Muckenkogel, 19 March 1935—a course for a 'Giant Gated Race', from the Cabana Marmolata (10,600 feet) to the Fedaja Saddle (6,500 feet), involving a drop of nearly 4,000 feet in a run of just over 3 miles. There were 50 gates, marked by staves 6 feet high, 18 to 25 yards apart. In this way yet another idea of Zdarsky's was revived and made a permanent asset for skiers. Neither Lunn nor Langes appear to have heard of their predecessor's preparatory work.

Ski-bunnies. The 'ski-bunny' at Rödöy in Norway is at least four thousand years old. This rock-drawing (Plate 122) shows a rabbit-hunter with his wooden missile and a rabbit-mask supposed to give him magical powers over his intended prey. He stands lightly poised forwards on long boards, whose points are curved broadly upwards, while their ends are slightly curved, to permit of running backwards. These primitive skis show tension and thus a highly-developed piece of equipment. The little man is 6 inches tall, his skis 13 inches long.

The 'ski-bunny' in Plate 123 is saying: 'Lord, how fine and healthy this is! If only it doesn't go out of fashion again!' The drawing is by F. V. Reznicek and appeared in *Simplicissimus* in 1908.

122

123

Matthias Zdarsky was known as the father of alpine ski-techniques. In his text-book, *The* (*Lilienfeld*) *Alpine Technique of Ski-running: an introduction to self-instruction*, he wrote: 'Anyone who follows my precepts exactly can master his skis sufficiently in two to four days to enable him to cope with every kind of ground.' From the 1908 edition we have taken four pictures: 'Running-turn' (Plate 124), 'About-turn' (125), 'Fall-position' (126) and 'Rescue position' (127). As long ago as 1898 Zdarsky founded an 'Alpine Ski-Club' (by 1912 it had 1575 members) and introduced the first 'gated race' in the history of ski-ing. It took place on 19 March 1905 on the Muckenkogel, near Lilienfeld. Plate 129 is part of a photograph which accompanied the publicity material for the race, definitely an instructional picture, showing Zdarsky with his 7 ft 3 ins skis in front of one of the numbered 'gates' on the course.

In 1904 the 'Nordic Games' at Mürzzuschlag were advertised by an early poster (Plate 128). This poster is a prize exhibit in Mürzzuschlag's interesting ski-museum. When the First World War started, the sport was turned to sterner uses; indeed, ski-courses were part of army-training before the outbreak. Plate 130 was taken on the alpine front, at the Passo di Paradiso. Soldiers breaking knee-deep through soft snow soon learned the advantages of the 'boards' in the snows of the high Alps.

128

◀ 124 125
126 127

129

130

'Wunder des Schneeschuhs' (Snowshoe Marvels) was the name not only of Arnold Fanck's ski-ing film, but also of a book he published in 1925, containing 1400 pictures selected from more than 2,000,000 frames in 25 miles of film! Plates 137–141, taken from that book, reveal what marvellous fun people were already finding in ski-ing at the time and how amusingly ski-books were already being illustrated.

Plate 135 shows the Arlberg area near St Christoph in 1902. It was then that the Alpine Club inaugurated a ski-ing course for guides, with the object of 'introducing the ski into the mountains in a uniform manner'. The head instructor, Wilhelm Paulcke, gave this account of an ascent of the Valluga: 'At first the attitude of the guides towards the undertaking was not exactly enthusiastic: in their view this was no place for ski-runners, but for step-cutting without skis, and one of them went so far as to pronounce that this was "the bloodiest nonsense he had ever seen in his life".' But, once on the summit they were all wildly excited; not one of the guides had ever been on top of a mountain in winter before.

The achievements of the ski-pioneers are hardly accorded their true value today, when ski-ing seems second nature. Among them was the creator of Sherlock Holmes, Sir Arthur Conan Doyle, who crossed the Maienfelder Furka from Davos to Arosa in 1894 on skis (Plate 131); 132 shows Wilhelm Paulcke; 133, Georg Bilgeri; 134, Hannes Schneider, the protagonist of the Arlberg technique of ski-ing.

'On the edge of the abyss', an illustration from Fridtjof Nansen's *Across Greenland on Snowshoes*, shows a 'stick-Telemark' halt in a dangerous situation (Plate 136). This book gave an immense impetus to ski-ing in the Alps.

131 133

132 134

135

136

137

138–141

The development of ski-ing. At the turn of the century it was generally accepted that one did not go up into the hills in winter. On 4 January 1896 five men tried to climb the 10,922-ft Oberalpstock in Switzerland on skis! 'Now the snow was no longer an enemy to be combated in a fierce, exhausting fight, which for so many had ended in their sinking, weary and worn-out, into the eternal sleep of that white bed. Now it had become our friend, revealing undreamed-of beauty and joy, even here, high in the mountains. Winged steps on our trusty "boards" bore us up, certain of victory, up and up into a marvellous winter sanctuary of the Alps. What a transformation the alpine winter was undergoing for humanity as it shed its unapproachable cruelty and showed its fair dazzling face, suffused with light and glory! And then we stood on the summit of the 10,922-ft Oberalpstock and sent out a ringing "Ski-Heil!" down into the valley. We had conquered the first alpine "Three-thousander" on skis!' Thus Wilhelm Paulcke in his book *Berge als Schicksal* (A Mountain Life). But he was wrong; for the first alpine 'Three-thousander' to be climbed on skis was the 10,234-ft Sonnblick, when Wilhelm v. Arlt got to its summit two years earlier.

All this was at the turn of the century. What an astonishing development from those days to the world-wide mass ski-ing of our own days (Plates 142–145)!

Overleaf: On skis in the Bernese Oberland today. Races at Grindelwald First, with the mighty Wetterhorn (12,150 ft) towering above the cloud sea, which fills the intervening valley.

142

143

145 ▶

144

20h-8h
V 21
647

After the Second World War skiing soon recovered and reached enormous momentum, particularly in North America and Japan; but the Alps still remained the outstanding centre of its development. This is true of technique, instructional methods and all forms of equipment with the exception of the American 'Head' ski.

Directly after the war it was the French who came to the fore in technique and instruction. The highly successful ski-racer Emile Allais evolved a *Méthode française de ski technique* in 1947, entirely based on the Austrian parallel-turn technique of Toni Seelos. In it he laid special emphasis on one detail in the slalom, the lifting of the ski-points during quick turns (*ruades*). But when the Austrian Instructional Plan came out in 1957, the Austrians resumed their leading position, even if the various 'weaving' schools in Switzerland and elsewhere refuse to acknowledge their indebtedness to Austria. Regular international conferences of ski-instructors are doing a great deal to coordinate methods of instruction.

The general development of technical aids was also brought into the service of teaching. Drag-lifts save beginners the time-wasting and exhausting business of climbing the slopes. Ropeways take classes up into snowy areas when the resort itself has none. This enables the pupil to learn as much in a day as he once did in a week. Admittedly the safety of the 'one-stick' days has never again been achieved. Accepting the fact that falls are bound to be more frequent using the two-stick technique, an attempt is at least being made to reduce the dangers of a fall by the use of safety bindings. Sideless bindings are the first real step forward since the spring-support, which a ski-jumper, Eng. Albert Bildstein, made in 1925, when in hospital after breaking a leg. Unfortunately, it is not so easy to find the right adjustment of safety bindings, and injuries to bones and tendons remain frequent. The field here is still wide open, but the position regarding ski-development is encouraging. Plastics and lamination have greatly improved springing, smoothness of gliding surface and durability. All the unpleasantnesses of loss of tension, warping and waxing have been eliminated with the coming of plastic soles.

And what are we to say about the ever-increasing numbers who go up by ropeway and run down on hard-packed runs, whose tally now exceeds that of the devotees of the old, enjoyable ski-touring? The founder of the Kandahar races, which means in effect of hard-*piste* downhill running, answers the question in these words: 'Downhill is a fine sport, but only a sport. Touring is an education, downhill a sign of the times.'

For Health's sake, string along! Instead of a smiling young lady, the Swiss National Tourist Office chose for their 1966–7 winter-sports poster a cheery old man with ancient skis. It proved one of the most successful touring posters ever.

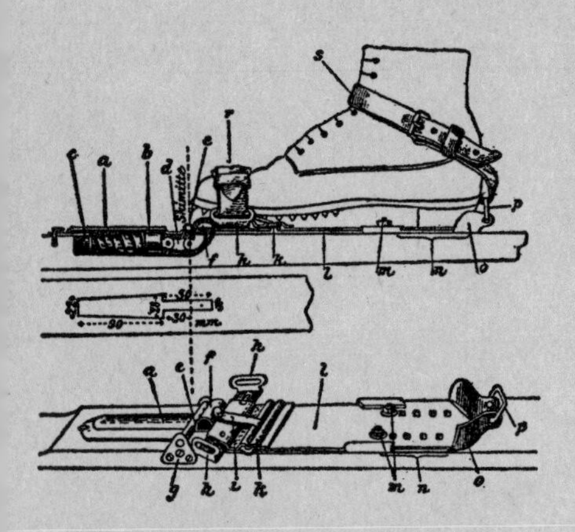

The Zdarsky Binding in 1896. a=tin cover; b=buffer-spring; c=control-screw; d=articulated rods; e=axis; f=toe-support; g=lateral grip; h=toe-clamps; i=toe-clamp bolt; k=sole-hinge; l=steel-sole; m=adjusting-screws; n=ankle-plate; o=heel-grip; p=base-buckle; r=toe-straps; s=instep-strap.

To put it differently: touring will always be the most satisfying aim, but where lack of time or opportunity makes it impossible, the ropeway and the lift will be gratefully accepted. In the end, figures speak for themselves: in 1960 Austria could boast 9 fixed cable-lifts and 68 aerial ropeways, capable of shifting 20,000 people an hour and actually transporting 16 million during that year. Add to these 68 new chair-lifts and 430 drag-lifts, transporting almost as many people, in fact 15 million, making around 30 million in all. The figure is an irrefutable indication of the importance and growth of the ski-cult in our own day. Even taking into account the fact that each skier travels many times by ropeway and lift in a winter's skiing and that this reduces the number of individual participants in the sport, it still amounts to a far larger figure than that of people who climb mountains during the summer.

The great movement for open-air sports, which originated in England in 1860, made us a present, as we have seen, of the equipment discovered by simple prehistoric Nordic hunters as a necessity of life. Very few people give a thought to the fact that they are lifted up into the mountains by the products of the most modern mechanization, to come charging down again a few minutes later on a stone-age invention.

A new migration of the tribes into the hills has begun, far greater than any undertaken in the past on foot. The ski has rendered accessible, in winter and spring, the world of the mountains, till now only to be invaded during the summer months. It is not too wide of the mark to speak of a 'rediscovery' of the mountains. Unlike mountaineering, it is quite impossible to envisage any limit to the growth of this new phenomenon—and that is perhaps the most cheering fact to emerge from this short excursion through the development of alpine skiing.

SPORT AMONG THE RAPIDS

Hans Kremslehner

Torrents and rapids are as much part of the mountains as snow and rock, and their negotiation is one of the many ways to enjoy the savage grandeur of the mountain scene.

The first to make their way, on swaying tree trunks lashed together, down alpine streams like the Isar, Salza and Enns (which are still Grade IV in today's six-grade scale of difficulty) were raftsmen using the mountain rivers as a traffic-highway, as also did the salt-boatmen. Rapid-riding, the third and latest form of alpine sport, following in the wake of climbing and skiing, at first lacked a suitable type of boat.

It was not till 1904 that the artist Charles Prelle brought over from America to Munich a collapsible boat very much like the Canadian Indians' canoes. Prelle, who did a ventriloquist's turn with his dog in a circus, had seen rafts on the Isar and had immediately risked the journey from Wolfratshausen to Munich in his fragile craft. The only other type of craft besides the Canadian canoe available, the kayak, was a product of northern huntsmanship and reached the peak of its development to technical perfection in South Greenland. These Eskimo boats were mentioned as far back as 1425 on a map of the Northlands drawn by the Dane, Clavus. Almost at the same time as Prelle, a French-Canadian called Smith also brought a Canadian canoe over and exhibited it in Paris to those interested. It was not long before the numerous easier rivers of France were being navigated in this type of boat.

In 1905 a student called Heurich saw an Eskimo kayak exhibited at Munich, which inspired him to build a collapsible boat of his own. His basic concept, to apply the technical principle of the Gothic pointed-arch to boat-building, was such a stroke of genius that all collapsible boats to this day have faithfully followed his contribution to their design. He is the father of the modern collapsible boat and therefore of the alpine sport of rapid-water canoeing. All he wanted at the time was a boat he could take to pieces so that he could more easily go fishing in the many recesses of the pools below the line of weirs behind his parents' house!

A Rosenheim tailor, Hans Klepper, saw Heurich's boat, immediately realized its immense possibilities, bought the patent from him and plunged into boat-building like a man possessed. He improved the collapsible in various details and also built a two-man collapsible for double-canoeing. These boats were still exclusive sporting equipment for a handful of canoe-enthusiasts; it was not till the enthusiastic descriptions given by C. J. Luther, a well-known climber and skier, that the appeal of the collapsible canoe was spread further afield. Suddenly these fragile-looking craft, which contemporaries labelled 'tatter-boats' or 'floating coffins', were to be seen everywhere.

The real development of rapids-navigation now began in the Western and Eastern Alps alike, in France as the Canadian canoes gained swift popularity, in Munich and Vienna owing to daring exploits in kayaks. About the time of the First World War, there lived in Vienna an ambitious Commissar of Police, who had plenty of spare time; this was Johannes Pietschmann, who gained his early experience with the unstable canoe on quiet waters; then, full of the zeal for adventure, graduated to more and more difficult streams, much to the discomfort of his superior officers, after which he gave innumerable thrilling lectures about his adventures. Pietschmann was a courageous pioneer on the Enns below Hieflau, on the Inn from Landeck down, on the Drave and on the Mur.

When three devotees of a sport get together, they found a club! While the 'Schnecke' was born at Linz in 1907, as Central Europe's first kayak club, Munich saw the origin of the first collapsible-canoe club in the world in 1912. One of the founders of the 'Schnecke' was Weinzinger, who built his so-called 'Linzer Schnecken' on the pattern of the Eskimo kayak, but of very narrow beam (they were about 18 inches broad and 6 to 7 feet long). Very soon these were quite at home on the foaming waters of the Enns.

In 1924 the Committee of the Austrian Kayak Association, with a view to unifying the proliferating types of boat, laid down measurements, which were to prove a hindrance to the development of canoeing on more difficult reaches. The restriction to boats of uniform width, as laid down, resulted in a definite standstill in the progress of the technique of canoeing in rapid waters, and Grade IV of the present six-grade scale of difficulty then seemed the most that man would ever be able to achieve in so fragile a craft.

But young men do not like to be confined by rigid systems. E. H. Pawlata, of Vienna, wrote: 'The collapsible is a monstrosity! A definite monstrosity! It is neither a Canadian nor a kayak!' He was determined to find the ideal boat for canoeing in rapids and, after much experimenting he decided on the 'Genuine Eskimo Kayak', about 38 inches broad and 18 feet long. Undeterred by the jeers and laughter of his friends, he next began trying to 'Eskimo', in other words to right the canoe by the use of the paddle after capsizing, a process about which as long ago as 1792 S. J. Baumgarten had written, in a book about America: 'Since they fear not the force of the water, nay, to take their pleasure therein, they do oft-times overset their *canot* and therewith turn a somerset thrice or even four times.'

Pawlata went on trying and trying till, finally, on 30 July 1927, on the Weissensee in Carinthia, he became the first European to right himself with the aid of the paddle. He went on to perfect his technique so completely that he eventually performed the operation with a tile and even with nothing but his hands. At the kayak championships in Copenhagen he exhibited his extraordinary skill by 'out-Eskimoing' the Eskimo competitors who were taking part, righting himself more quickly and with less risk. To use a climbing metaphor, in so doing Pawlata had fashioned the 'belaying-rope of rapid-canoeing', and given a fresh impulse to the technique and exploitation of the sport on the most difficult of rivers.

Among the Eastern Alps, the chief devotees to take up the new sport on ever more raging waters with zeal and enthusiasm—most of them had been climbers or skiers of note—were Alber, Gamerith, Walleczek, Kronfeld and Hromatka. As in mountaineering, the 'thirties saw an undreamed-of development in technique, which made significant performances possible. The economic crisis had reached its worst point. The dreams and hopes of the younger generation remained unfulfilled, so they went after new targets, far beyond the scope of ordinary, everyday life. The youth of the day decided to climb the most horrific precipices and tame the most savagely broken waters of mountain streams, seeking in these pursuits to justify their existence by fighting nature herself and the might of her elements.

By 1932 most of the alpine torrents and streams had succumbed to adventurous canoeists. There remained only the upper reaches, mostly encumbered by boulders, a small number of 'super-severe' stretches, such as the Klausenkofel on the Möll, the Salzachöfen, the gateway of the Gesäuse, the Kummerbrücken reach of the Enns, and a few streams like the Lieser in Carinthia.

The time had come when climbers were to attempt and master the north faces of the Zinne and Eiger, canoeists the Salzachöfen. The latter, a stretch where the Salzach forces a gorge-like passage through sheer rock below the Lueg Pass is, like the Eigerwand, more dangerous than technically difficult. Its conditions can be altered in an instant by minimal changes in the water-level, while fierce undercurrents and the huge undercut faces of the cliffs are a positive nightmare for everyone who attempts this perilous passage. The first to negotiate this thundering hell of white, foam-lashed waters was the incredibly youthful

The Salzachöfen Gorges near Golling, whose exit is shown in Plate 148, are rated by rapids-enthusiasts much the same as the north face of the Eiger by climbers: a highly perilous undertaking. A memorial tablet on the path leading the tourist into the dark 'Dom', from which he can look down on the raging waters of the river, here confined to a breadth of a few yards, reminds him of the first descent of the Salzachöfen in a kayak. This daring achievement fell to a student from Vienna, Adolf Anderle (Plate 147), on 6 September 1931. Only a few months later, on 13 February 1932, he met with a fatal accident on a harmless ski outing.

The Salzachöfen rapids are still classified as Grade VI in the canoeists' scale of difficulty. Franz Alber, who negotiated them successfully much later, deeply impressed with the objective dangers of the passage, wrote: 'Canoeing skill has only a very minor part to play in coming through safely here.'

147

148 ▼

149

A rapid-water canoeist in the Salzach Gorge (Plate 151), and another in Verdon Gorge (153). The latter is 20 miles long and situated in the French Alps. Its passage is a splendid venture and can, according to water-conditions and the canoeist's skill, take anything from six hours to four days.

Besides 'canoe-hiking', competitive canoeing in the rapids gives pleasure to many devotees. Plate 149 shows the first woman to compete in one of these regattas, held on the Isar in about 1924 (Bad Tölz–Munich). Plate 152 is a photograph taken during a rapid-water slalom on the Steyr in 1966.

The adoption of 'Eskimoing'– the ability to right oneself after capsizing – came as the ultimate boon to rapid-water canoeists. In his book, *Kipp Kipp Hurra!*, Edi Hans Pawlata wrote with due pride: 'On 30 July 1927, against all the expectations of experienced paddlers, I became the first European sportsman to right myself after capsizing.' And he goes on: 'The ability to right oneself is the basic skill of the real kayak sport.' Plate 150 shows Pawlata as he 'Eskimoed' on that memorable day. No other than the great Fridtjof Nansen autographed the photograph with these words: 'I was most interested to learn the degree to which the kayak sport has been developed so far from its land of origin.'

150

Mir ist es sehr interessant gewesen zu erfahren wie gut sich der Kajaksport so weit von seiner Heimat entwickelt hat.
Mit den besten Wünschen für die Zukunft
Fridtjof Nansen

151 152

'Kayak-canoeing at its highest sporting level', writes Herbert Rittlinger, the collapsible-boat pioneer, 'takes us into a primeval landscape. It can, at times, even take us into the Absolute Landscape. This, I claim, is something which with two exceptions – genuine exploration and true mountaineering – only the collapsible-boat can do for us.'

The picture shows collapsible canoes in the 1,000-ft-deep gorges of the Var in the French Alps. At one point the red bauxite of its containing walls closes in to a width of only 6 yards – a veritable gorge of Hell!

Viennese schoolboy Adolf Anderle, who was a fearless, adventurous and ambitious performer, and an enthusiastic hand at 'Eskimoing'. On 6 September 1931, he was the first ever to succeed in this hazardous enterprise, using his Eskimo kayak, which he had christened 'Fram' after Nansen's world-famous ship. Even before this single-handed effort he had collected a number of 'first-ever' successes.

He was followed by almost every member of the canoeing *élite* of the day, and the 'Öfen' handled them all pretty roughly. Frühwirth was dashed against the face of the cliffs and had to negotiate the last part of the cataract stern-first; Dr Walleczek, who went solo (of all things!) in a two-man Klepper-canoe, capsized under the 'Dome' and only reached safety in a quiet backwater behind a huge boulder, since named 'Walleczek's Harbour', by the most strenuous efforts; Gamerith overturned and had to swim the whole stretch to the end of the gorge, where he was picked out of the water unconscious. When he opened his eyes his first words were: 'Water, give me water: I'm thirsty!' Alber, on his third trip, was flung out of his craft by the incredible fury of the waters, but somehow managed to reach the 'Walleczek Harbour', where he clung to the ice-cold rock for two hours, till an alpine rescue-team from Golling roped him up out of the gorge.

After 1932 the spread of canoeing everywhere reached a totally unforeseen peak of development. The Austrian Kayak Association sent out 20,000 pamphlets in three languages, advertising the delights of touring on swift-flowing streams, and instituted 'river-guides' and training-tours on the lines of similar mountaineering products. The 'extremists', with Dr Hromatka in the van, drafted out a six-grade scale of difficulty, which was soon accepted internationally and remains standard everywhere today.

At that time, the centres of swift-current canoeing were France, whose Canadian-canoe specialists were putting up fabulous performances and, in Austria, the 'Munich' and 'Vienna' schools, as well as the highly progressive 'Hochschulring Deutscher Kayakfahrer'. This period of development reached its zenith before the Second World War, when F. von Alber canoed the River Lieser and its fearsome gorge in three and a half days, a feat about which he remarked: 'You would be hard put to it not to be bashed to pieces if you turned over.'

All the tours among the Eastern Alps were made in collapsibles or kayaks, but in France the collapsible has never yet become at all popular. Yet it was a Viennese exponent of collapsible-canoeing, Robert Kronfeld, who, as long ago as the 'twenties, was the first, only and last canoeist to ride the waters of the Rhone Gorge below Geneva; for, today, a huge reservoir fills that great rift and the *Perte du Rhône*, which was once its feature, where the whole stream vanished into its own rocky bed, to gush out again after pursuing a subterranean course for a few yards. No object sucked into the *Perte du Rhône* was ever seen again.

Once canoeing on ordinary waters in 'Canadians' had become popular in France, the opening up and exploration of the lovely rapid-flowing streams in this western sector of the Alps by French devotees of this type of boat began soon after 1930. In the years before the war they negotiated the mighty waters of the Isère, which rises south of Mont Blanc; the Cheran, outstanding in its scenic as well as its sporting attractions; and the impressive Gorges of the Drac, carving their way at a terrifying depth through the rock. At the same time the Durance, with its mighty current and the great gorges of the Verdon and the Var, in the farthest angle of the great curve of the Alps, were opened up. The 'Grand Canyon of the Verdon' is one of Europe's most magnificent gorges and still constitutes for the rapid-water canoeist a 20-mile rift, with numerous difficult *portages* and rock-pitches to be climbed, remote from the world in its deep-cut gorges, of the utmost severity and hazard. The Gorge of the Var, carving its way 1,000 feet deep into the dark-red bauxite of its containing faces is still considered the finest, most difficult and treacherous of all the French gorges; for the rains generated by thunderstorms can with incredible rapidity alter the level of its waters by several metres and so turn the rift into a death-trap.

Another development before the Second World War was the simultaneous but independent introduction in Switzerland and Austria of the 'slalom'. A Viennese called Rabe sketched out the first plan for a canoeing-slalom on his ticket during a tram-journey, and it actually took place on the Mühltraisen in 1934. The 'gates' were marked by red and green stakes and the underlying idea was described as 'the mastery of the boat among rapids'—a kind of school in canoeing technique! This aspect of rapid-water canoeing was taken up enthusiastically, parallel with down-stream racing among the rapids, and nowadays world-championships are held every two years.

After the war, there was little new water left for the adventurous young canoeist; all that is available are a few probably impossible reaches of existing rivers and the head-waters of a small number of streams, even higher up than heretofore. To attempt such reaches in a collapsible is sheer boat-slaughter, though science has come to the rescue here, as it has in mountaineering with the nylon-fibre rope, by providing Polyester and Epoxi-resins for boat-building. The manufacture of these plastic boats is very easy compared with the building of collapsibles, which requires a considerable degree of technical skill; the materials are cheap, repairs easily effected, without the need for workshops. The transport of such a boat, on the other hand, is a much more complicated affair.

In addition to reaches only suitable for these plastic boats—the so-called 'Polyester-streams', with their wet stones and rock-steps—paddlers with an urge for exploration have discovered and mastered a number of splendid new reaches of the known rivers. Among these is the 20-mile-long rift, through forests and rock-walls, hidden away in the southernmost tip of Austria, the gorges of the Gail; as also the famous, and indeed fearsome, 'Gesäuse Gateway' on the Enns, of which the one-time canoe-champion of the rapids, Hromatka, wrote in 1936 that it would probably never be mastered. But a new generation discovered and solved these few remaining problems. That marked the end of the wonderful era of discovery and the romance of pioneering; the splendid adventure of rapid-water canoeing still offers its thrills. Rapids rise and fall; for the man in the little boat they are always new, always different. And today, in spite of the proliferation of hydro-electric installations, there are still sufficient unspoiled mountain streams for exciting ventures on foaming waters.

A newspaper advertisement for collapsible canoes in 1907.

BUILDING IN THE ALPS

Willi End

In 1906 two Zürich engineers applied for a permit to build a railway to the top of the Matterhorn. An electric line was to take passengers up to the Swiss Alpine Club's hut at over 10,000 feet, from where a funicular would carry them onwards inside the mountain (its maximum gradient 95%) to the 14,782-foot Swiss summit. There, it was planned to build a pressurized observation-room, to spare the tourists the discomforts of mountain-sickness. Climbers were quick to protest against this project, and even non-mountaineers raised their voice against it. *Alpina*, the S.A.C's journal, commented: 'How many are likely to climb the Matterhorn any more, once they know that, as a reward for their exertions, they will have the pleasure of joining an international company of trippers, some of them comfortably installed in a goggle-box, others devoting their attention to the defaced and depreciated last few feet of the summit?' That particular Matterhorn railway was not built.

When, at the end of the last century, a plan was set afoot to build a railway up Vienna's Schneeberg, every Viennese mountaineer promptly refused to allow such a thing. Nonetheless, it was built and 1897 saw its opening. Nine years later a climber wrote in the mountain periodical *Der Gebirgsfreund*: 'The railway goes to the top of the hill which, to many a walker, is an abomination. However, though opinions are still divided, it is beyond doubt that we have gradually accustomed ourselves to the spectacle of man's hand being raised everywhere in conflict with Nature; and where this conflict takes such substantial shape as the building of a mountain railway we cannot conceal our recognition of such feats and we are compelled to marvel when we suddenly see the narrow strip of track penetrating the mountain wilderness. Indeed, we stop and listen, wondering whether the noisy, snorting monster, which has in our day replaced the fiery dragons of legendary ages, will come to disturb for a short time the magic silence of the mountain world, only to leave it more impressive after the loud-voiced monstrosity has disappeared from our sight. And so, we will surely get used to the railway up the Schneeberg, too. It is only a matter of time before it will become identified in our imagination with the mountain, and we shall come to regard its curves, viaducts and tunnels as quite natural features and challenging to our imagination.' When, sixty years later, the rumour went abroad that the old Schneeberg cog-wheel railway was to be replaced by a modern cable-railway, all the mountaineers in Vienna were outraged . . . 'The Schneeberg,' they lamented, 'won't be our old Schneeberg without the cog-wheel railway!'

Yes, he was right. We have got so used to 'seeing man's hand raised in conflict with Nature' that marked paths, mountain railways, the alpine passes, huts and refuges all seem the most natural things in the world. And it is these items which have, during the past hundred years, thrown open the Alps to the travelling public.

Before that time, there were occasional paths up to the high pastures on the Alps. Beyond them, narrow hunting-tracks led up into the cwms above. The first paths to actual summits were built by philanthropists at their own expense, as for instance the Stüdlweg, built on the Grossglockner in 1879 by Johannes Stüdl and the path up the Wischberg in 1874, the work of Gustav Jäger.

Similarly, the first refuges in the high Alps were built privately. The inn built on the 8,803-foot Faulhorn in Switzerland in 1831 was for years the most loftily situated house in Europe. Zermatt's first hotel was built in 1852. The first mountain refuge built by an Alpine Club was the Grünhornhütte (8,036 feet) at the eastern foot of the Tödi. In his circular

The Gotthard Railway at a point near Göschenen. The train speeds high above gorges and houses. This exaggerated picture speaks for the pride men felt in the nineteenth century at the achievements of science. The railway was opened in 1882.

addressed to 'Climbers and Mountain-lovers in Switzerland', which led to the foundation of the Swiss Alpine Club, Theodor Simler wrote, as propaganda for its construction: 'High up in the mountains, there are numerous phenomena, some physical, some chemical and geological, to be studied; the pursuit of these studies is often made difficult by the conditions encountered on the spot, and the expense is an additional hardship. Were the Association to take over the siting of huts in specially interesting locations, its members who are engaged in research of this kind would be greatly assisted; moreover, artists, photographers and others would be enabled to make longer sojourns at points of especial beauty. At the moment we

Mountain paths. The first sign-posts in the mountains were stones laid on top of each other. Such 'stone-men' (cairns) are still built on trackless ground: big ones, little ones, and there is scarcely a climber whom one of them has not brought back from the rock-wilderness onto a proper track and so spared him a bivouac or even worse. Stone-men have a magic of their own; climbers love them.

As the number of climbers grew, the Alpine Clubs began to improve, extend and mark the paths to the refuges and beyond them towards the summits. The German and Austrian Alpine Club installed 2,500 sign-boards in a single year, 1908. Literally tons of iron went up into the mountains in the shape of iron ladders, stakes and cables. In 1843 the route up the Dachstein was safeguarded with iron stakes and ropes: the first 'prepared' rock-climb in the eastern Alps. Members of the Imperial House and noblemen like Count Metternich provided the money. It had become a matter of honour to take part in the opening-up of the mountains.

It is not only a mint of money but the voluntary work of many an idealist which has gone into the network of paths from the Mediterranean to the Vienna Woods. Few ever think of them. The path-conservers and marking-parties are the most unobtrusive members of every Alpine Club.

155

156

157

The alpine passes. Before the first ascent of Mont Blanc, a crossing of the Gotthard Pass was considered the 'peak of alpine adventure'. Schiller called the passage of the Schöllenen Gorge a 'road of terror', and it was as such that the periodical *Über Land und Meer* pictured it (Plate 158) as late as 1874, by which time a perfectly good road had been built. Plate 162 is an engraving from the middle of the 19th century showing the Val Tremola (the Valley of Shivers) on the south side of the pass*; 161 is an original photograph of the old horse-drawn postal diligence. On the post's inaugural journey over the pass, 78 men stood by at the danger-points to replace the coach and carry the mail to the next carriageable section. In 1780 a traveller mentions the Loibl Pass (Plate 159), the construction of which began in 1717, as a 'beautiful, costly road'; but he complained bitterly about its steepness.

The first 'touring-road' was the Dolomitenstrasse, the great series of linked passes through the heart of the Dolomite ranges. It was thrown open to traffic in 1909 'in order to unlock the Dolomites to the great flood of travellers'. Plate 160 is from a picture-book with photographs by Fritz Benesch, which appeared in the same year to popularize the road. It will be seen that Wordsworth's cachet of 'the lonely hills' still applied then to the Dolomite Road.

* Since mid-1967, the famous windings of the Val Tremola are a hazard of the past. A superb four-lane motorway, high on 'stilts', swings down the southern face of the Gotthard in three easily-graded, long 'dog-legs' to replace the former notorious bottleneck on which the traffic piled up bumper to bumper for hours on end, especially at week-ends. *(Translator's note.)*

◄ 158

159

160 ▲ 161

162

The alpine passes are taken for granted today. In the last century they ranked as 'miracles of engineering' and as memorials 'far outstripping the pyramids and temples of antiquity'.

The Great St Bernard Pass (8,114 ft) is clear of snow for only three months in the year. Even after the road had been built, its passage was often an exciting venture. Plate 164, a mid-19th century picture, may seem exaggerated now; but the morgue at the St Bernard Hospice, where those who had perished of exposure or exhaustion, or overwhelmed by avalanches, were laid out, was filled with victims even in our own century. The new road tunnel, 1,000 ft below the summit of the old pass, opened in 1966, obviates past hardships and dangers.

The opening in 1866 of the Furka Pass, which skirts the very edge of the Rhone Glacier, was a first-class sensation for alpine voyagers. Plate 163 shows riders crossing the pass – a favourite holiday pursuit of the day, especially enjoyed by British visitors.

The Grossglockner Road is held by many to be the finest of all (Plate 165). Work on the route began in 1924, when it was soon discovered that there had once been an ancient Roman road over the pass, its traces overgrown but still clearly identifiable.

163

165 ▸

164

Mountain railways. The Semmeringbahn, built between 1848 and 1854, was the first railway in the Alps. It was built at a time when, elsewhere, trains were hauled up specially steep places by horses. There were no prototypes for the tracing of the route for this mountain railway, and when it was begun there did not even exist a steam-engine which could have negotiated its gradients. The opening of the line was a triumph, and the eighteen lithographs made by Imre Benkert on the order of Emperor Franz Joseph I are redolent of the pride felt in this great technical achievement. Plate 166 shows the building of one of the viaducts. But, for the neighbouring mountain peasants, the railway was for a long time a 'work of the devil'; they crossed themselves whenever a train came along.

It took 2,392 working-days, from 1895 to 1906, before the first train ran through the Simplon Tunnel, over twelve miles long. Its cost was 87,000,000 gold francs and 39 lives. Plate 167 shows water bursting into the workings during construction.

After the end of the Second World War, work started on the Mont Blanc Ropeway, dubbed 'the Eighth Wonder of the World'. Its completion has made it possible to cross the Mont Blanc group from Italy to France, or vice versa, in the gondolas of the cable system, borne high above the glaciers. Plate 168 shows work inside the vertical face of the Aiguille du Midi during the building of Europe's highest ropeway-station, at 12,500 ft. From the halfway exchange station at Plan de l'Aiguille, the longest single cable-ropeway span in the world carries the forty-passenger cars 5,000 ft to the top.

166

167

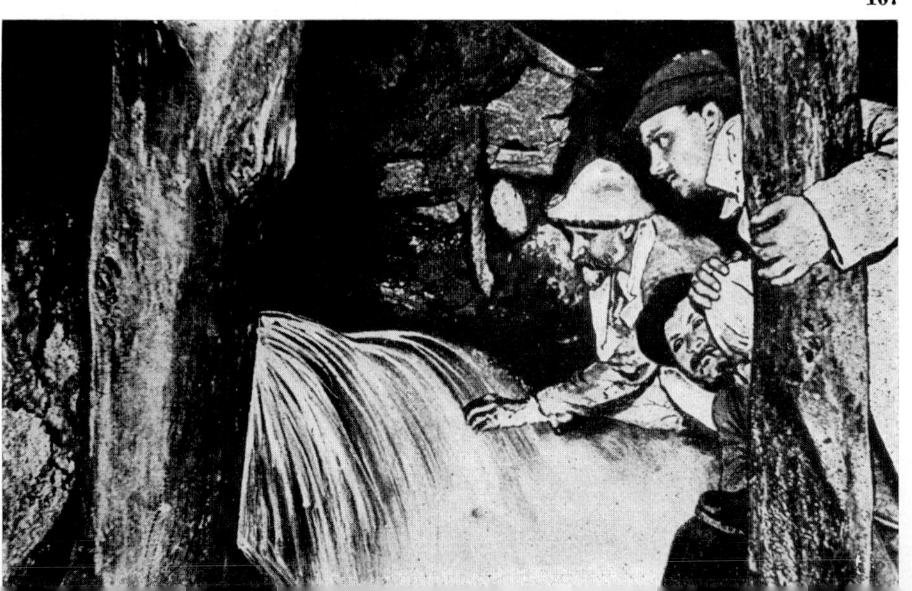

168 ▶

Mountain railways. The Rigibahn, opened in 1871 (Plate 170), was the first railway to go to an actual summit. One of the most hair-raising railways over a pass was the Mont-Cenis Railway, completed in 1860 (Plate 169). On its run down to the valley, passengers used to shut their eyes, in fear of their lives. According to Whymper it required much courage to be a driver on this line.

Towards the end of the last century, a project was mooted for a railway to the summit of the Jungfrau. The idea was to force the passengers to the top by compressed air, like letters in a postal tube, in a cylinder capable of holding fifty people, up a lined tunnel 10 ft broad. Theodor Wundt wrote about this project: 'a whole year's unblemished accident-free operation would be required to inspire public confidence and to banish the fear that one might either get stuck half-way up the tunnel owing to some unexpected intervention of friction, or be suddenly thrown to the bottom entrance again because the air pressure failed.' It took from 1896 to 1912 to build the Jungfrau Railway in its present form, up into the Jungfraujoch's icy world (Plate 174). The key to Plate 172, which shows Europe's highest railway station at the Joch, is as follows: 1. Jungfraujoch station (11,339 ft). 2. Hotel and panoramic terrace. 3. Lift. 4. Restaurant. 5. Path to the Plateau. 6. Ice-palace. 7. Entrance to the Sphinx tunnel. 8. Tourist accommodation. 9. International Research Institute 10. Sphinx tunnel. 11. Sphinx lift. 12. Sphinx terraces, 11,719 ft. 13. Exit from Sphinx tunnel. 14. Polar dogs and ski-school.

However, not every scheme of this technological age has come to fruition. An example was the concession granted in 1890 for a railway from Heiligenblut to the Adlersruhe (Grossglockner, Plates 171 and 173), which was never built.

169

171 173
172 174 ▸

170

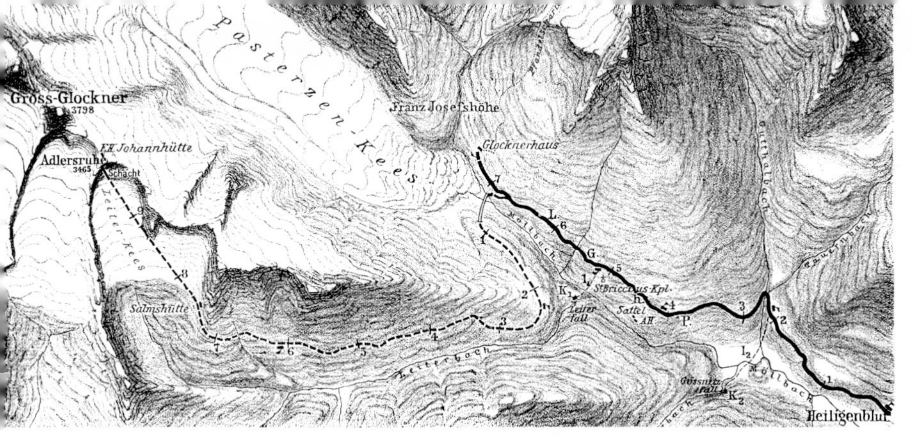
Pasterzen Kees
Gross-Glockner
3798
Franz Josefshöhe
Glocknerhaus
Erzh. Johannhütte
Adlersruhe
3465
Schacht
Leiter Kees
Möllbach
Gutthalbach
St. Briccius Kpl.
Salmshütte
Leiterfall
Sattel
Leiterbach
Gössnitz Fall
Möllbach
Heiligenblut

JUNGFRAUJOCH
3454 m 11.333 ft.

From bivouacs to mountain hotels. Modern refuges like the Rudolfshütte, shown in Plate 175, tend to let us forget how unpretentious the early mountaineers were. Plate 176 shows the interior of an old refuge in winter. The picture was taken in 1934 on the first ski traverse of the Alps from Vienna to Mont Blanc, which took five months, by Sepp Brunhuber and Julia Huber.

Franz Josef Hugi, the natural-historian, erected a primitive stone shelter on the Unteraar Glacier to further his researches (Plate 177). From 1840 to 1845 Louis Agassiz and several other professors lived in it for a few weeks every summer, after improving it slightly, and were perfectly satisfied with their primitive stone house, which made their scientific work possible. They spread straw on the slate slabs and put a wax-sheet over it; such were the beds of these learned gentlemen. A blanket served as a door and the kitchen was under the overhang of a boulder nearby; the daily menu was almost invariably limited to rice and mutton. At night, when the temperature fell sharply, they slept with their chickens. Preserving their sense of humour throughout, the dons christened their bivouac-hut the 'Hôtel des Neuchâtelois'.

Josef Enzensperger, the first weather-man at the meteorological station opened on the summit of the Zugspitze in 1900, felt like a soldier in a forward observation post (Plates 178, 179). This is what he wrote: 'If my ultimate successor should happen to have little mountain knowledge and experience, the best advice I can give him is to shut himself for six or seven months after the first big snowfall inside the tower; a condition whose acceptability, or even its endurability, gives food for controversy.'

175

176

177

178 179

Mountain refuges. The first shelter at high altitudes was a stone hut, which Saussure had built in 1785 in the glacier area of Mont Blanc. Today the highest alpine hut is the Capanna Margherita on Monte Rosa's Signalkuppe (14,960 ft). Plate 180 shows the material for its interior furnishing being carried up in 1892; and the following year the hut was thrown open in the presence of the Queen of Italy.

On the Matterhorn's Swiss (Hörnli) Ridge stands the Solvay Refuge, a refuge in the truest sense of the word (Plate 182). Does anyone today give a thought to the difficulties under which huts like this were built? When Guido Rey climbed the Matterhorn in 1893, the no less exposed Amadeo Hut was being built on the Italian face of the peak. Rey realized 'what toil and sweat the building of these little shelters on that mighty mountain had cost the men who put them there'. He further reports: 'Some of the workmen had been eyewitnesses only a few days before of the fatal accident to young Seiler and his famous guide Biener, quite close to the hut. They recalled that they had themselves negotiated the spot where the disaster happened at least fifty times, and carrying on their shoulders, at that, the beams for the refuge. They were quite incapable of understanding how such a fatality could have occurred. The two men had simply disappeared from sight, roped together, without uttering a sound; the only noise had been that of the stones they had carried away with them, clattering up from the depths far below... They spoke of these things calmly and quietly, as men who live their lives face to face with the elements do, completely resigned to the dictates of fate.'

180

182 ▸

181

The Alps by air. At the beginning of this century, it became fashionable to float high above the Alps in balloons. There was even an 'Association for Air-tours in Tyrol', founded at Innsbruck in 1910, which hired out the balloons; the charge for the hire of a balloon filled with lighting-gas was 600 Kroner. 'It was like being carried from one mountain peak to another by some superhuman power', wrote A. W. Andernach after his flight from Innsbruck to the north face of the Montasch. 'If one takes into account the majestic, glorious peace and silence of the high places, so precious to us mountaineers, undisturbed by the tiniest whisper of a wind (for in a balloon, of course, one floats on the wind itself) it will be understood that I can only compare our condition with that of happy intoxication.'

In 1910 the Peruvian airman Geo Chavez piloted a powered airship across the Simplon from Brig to Domodossola. Though he was killed while trying to land, he was long honoured in aviation circles as 'the conqueror of the Alps'. In 1925, the first attempt at an alpine air-rescue was made in the Bernina Group with an aeroplane. For many years, the Swiss Hermann Geiger operated his rescue service by plane, saving innumerable lives before he was killed while taking off. Nowadays, the helicopter, from which rescuers are winched down to retrieve victims of accidents, has become the aircraft of the Alps (Plate 184). In 1962, the Valaisian parachutist Erich Felbermayr jumped down onto the summit of the Traunstein – the first alpine summit to be landed on by parachute. In 1965, he jumped from the summit of the Kleine Zinne into the void (Plate 185), to test out 'further possibilities of parachute jumping among the high peaks', with an application to mountain rescue work; but he was also driven by a purely sporting motive, the desire to 'make that old, old dream come true, for a man just to hurl himself into the depths from a mountain peak and then float safely down to earth' (Wolf Weitzenböck).

OVERLEAF: A great rock climb, the 'Via delle Bocchette' in the Brenta Dolomites.

◀ 183

184 ▼

185 ▶

only mention the Tödi, on whose summit-ridge many would gladly have spent a whole day, had there been the certainty of finding protection against the cold of the night, say, at about the level of the Yellow Cliff.'

The huts built in those days were small and simply-equipped—refuges pure and simple. The rules of the Swiss Alpine Club in 1886 laid down the minimum inventory for such a refuge: 'Sufficient dry hay or straw on the sleeping-boards; 1 blanket for each person finding a place there; 1 cooking-stove; 2 cooking-pots; 1 ladle; 1 soup bowl; 1 coffee-can or pot; 1 soup-plate for each person; 1 spoon each; a few forks; ditto knives; 1 cup each; 1 slop pail; a table and bench; a chair or stool; a box or canteen for the cutlery; 1 broom; 1 lantern with candles or oil, if appropriate; 1 axe; 1 set of the hut-regulations; 1 visitors' book with pencil.'

That climbers were grateful for the presence of these huts, even if they were not always very comfortable to stay in, is confirmed by a report of Paul Güssfeld's in 1885. 'We usually spend the night before a big day,' he wrote, 'in a hut of some kind, a herdsman's maybe, or one of the refuges provided *ad hoc* for travellers. Most of these places of refuge stand between 6,500 and 10,000 feet, high up among the great peaks, far from any human habitation, often in magnificent situations, surrounded by glaciers and dominated by snow-spires and rock-teeth. This makes it most rewarding to spend two consecutive nights up there, devoting the intervening day to minor excursions. A rest-day of this kind high up in the hills permits of many observations which the exertions of a big venture would render impossible. Many a question comes to mind; our duty fully to comprehend the constituent features of this new, strange world becomes more keenly felt, our relationship with it deeper and stronger.

'The niggardly interior of these refuges has little relation to the magnificence of the world outside them. At night, inside one of them, by the light of a candle, everything looks sad indeed; this depressing effect can be greatly minimized by shouldering the very slight extra weight of half a dozen, or even a dozen, stearin-candles and burning them all at the same time.

'Nobody looks forward to going to bed; it is observed mainly as a duty. One could soon get used to one's uncomfortable "bed"; the oppressive atmosphere engendered by the presence of only a few people is quite a different matter. Then there are other things: the restless tossing and turning of one or another; the loud, regular snoring of some person who has managed to get to sleep; perhaps, too, one is worrying about the weather, or over-anxious in advance about how some unknown climb will go—all these things combine to keep one awake a very long time.'

Nowadays, the guest in a mountain hut, as elsewhere, demands his comfort. Where porters would once hump provisions and drinks up to the hut on his back, the helicopter is coming more and more into use; the guest, too, is more choosy about the menu. And the club committee-men have their share of worries. Most of the huts have reached a worthy old age (buildings age more rapidly in the mountains!); they are becoming dilapidated or are no longer large enough to house the growing flow of visitors. These huts are no longer an asset to the clubs, rather on the debit side of the sheet. Between 1948 and 1958, the Austrian Alpine Association spent nearly £500,000 on its huts alone! On top of this, the maintenance of the same club's network of paths, which has grown up over a whole century and is now 25,000 miles long (or the length of the Equator), required the expenditure of about £20,000 between 1950 and 1960. This was the cost of repairing 5,000 miles of path, marking or re-marking 14,000 miles, setting up 7,000 sign boards, providing 8,000 ski-markings. The actual expenditure was entirely absorbed by the materials—the work was done *gratis* by volunteers.

There have always been volunteers and philanthropists in the mountain-world. Examples are the monks in the hospices on the great alpine passes and the hosts of the Tauernhäuser, founded in the sixteenth century, whose duties were 'to keep open and in good repair the ways; the setting up of snow-poles and cairns of stones; to keep open their houses of refuge to every stranger; to accompany needy and sick travellers and furnish them with shelter and fare; the search for, rescue and restoration to well-being of those who had lost their way or suffered accident; as well as the transport of the bodies of those who had perished among the mountains to the nearest manse, and Christian burial there.'

There is still great loving-kindness in today's fulfilment of the mission 'to ease the difficulties of alpine travel'.

ARTISTS AND THE ALPS

Fritz Schmitt

'Art is the spice of life', a lover of the arts once proclaimed. Many climbers and lovers of the mountains will probably disagree; for them, the spice of life is the very opposite of art, artifice or artificiality—nature herself.

Nevertheless, it cannot be denied that there is a strong and valuable relationship between knowledge of the Alps, climbing among them, and the art that seeks to portray them. The old Viennese mountaineer Hans Wödl went so far as to claim that 'climbing is art', while the mountaineering painter Egon Hofmann-Linz gave a completely contrary definition: 'Art is not that which is beautiful, but that which achieves a powerful effect.'

Art is the expression of an experience realized, must always be and remains an expression of the times. It is precisely this that makes art interesting for any thoughtful mountaineer; for old maps, books, sketches and paintings provide him with a comprehensive survey of the past and, through their pictorial representations, reveal to him the development of the ability to see, comprehend and reproduce nature in all its forms. More than this, every work of art makes it possible to understand how earlier generations reacted to the surrounding landscape.

In his book about Expressionism, E. von Sydow wrote: 'There is no room for the production of a work except to heighten the feeling for life itself!'

Which brings us back to mountaineering.

The landscape-painter does not deal in topography or the geological structure of the Alps. He does not work to precise scientific standards and uses no complicated instruments for the reproduction of what his eye beholds. His materials and methods are almost primitively simple: a strip of canvas or cardboard, a pencil, paint-brushes and colours, and again colours . . . to these he brings a relaxed, creative hand, creative powers and the imponderable quality of imagination, from a combination of which elements he produces his true work of art.

Landscape painting has followed entirely different courses in the cultures of China and Europe. After an early dawn and sunset in antiquity, landscape in Europe was not consciously sought out, visualized and taken as a subject until the fifteenth century; thence, slowly, it was transformed from a mere background, a distinct back-cloth more especially to religious subjects until, in the nineteenth century, it became a subject in its own right. And as the attitude changed, so mountains, in the variety of their shapes, came into the focus of the painter's vision.

For the artists of Pompeii and Rome 'mountains represented the natural limit to the landscape . . . they were a frontier on the horizon, but part of the universal harmony of the earth, as were gardens, trees, quiet corners of the land, and the sea' (Ulrich Christoffel). We find mountains, too, later on (fifth to twelfth century AD) in the splendid Byzantine mosaics at Ravenna, as well as in the smaller art forms of Christian book-illustration, in Bibles, gospels and miniatures. True, the representation of mountains in these is far removed from actuality, varying from naïve attempts to picture cliffs and rock-steps, through pure symbolism, to mere abstractions.

In China, the art of the same era blossomed on very different lines. Chinese artists had a marvellous talent for depicting atmospheric effects, the clouds, mist and snow, with virtuoso skill. The mixture of realism and magic, of the physical and the spiritual eye, is staggeringly impressive. The art of the Far East is an art of delicate tones, not of violent colour-contrasts; it is content to use the most economical methods of representation. To describe landscape, the Chinese use the portmanteau-word *shan-shui*, literally 'mountain and water'.

Furthermore: 'the Far Eastern picture has neither a solid base nor a frame. It is painted on silk or on paper, which is then rolled up and only unrolled when someone wants to look at it' (Otto Fischer). So you get a highly cultivated approach both to the production of the picture and to the savouring of the picture produced.

Unfortunately, there is room within the scope of this article for only brief references in a somewhat restricted survey. The breadth and wealth of the artistic treasure under review makes the choice of works and the characterization of the artists equally difficult.

Anyone more deeply interested in the theme of mountains in pictures should refer to two books—both, alas, out of print—*Die Alpen und ihre Maler*, by E. W. Bredt, which came out before the First World War, and the Swiss Alpine Club's centenary publication in 1963, *Der Berg in der Malerei* by Ulrich Christoffel.

Bredt's book is comprehensive, but contains only black and white illustrations; it also includes graphic work. Some of the ideas developed are very personal. The review closes with the end of the nineteenth century.

Ulrich Christoffel, the historian of art, who lives in Chur, leaves a great many typical twentieth-century mountain painters, some of them quite important, without a mention in his recent book. There is not a word about Fritz Baer, Otto Bauriedl, Hans Herzing, Adalbert Holzer, Gustav Jahn, Otto Pippel, Ernst Platz, Alfons Walde and many others. In his book *Europäische Graphik im 19 Jahrhundert*, Claude Roger-Marx wrote, with a fine touch of irony: 'In the art world, the experts are always wrong!' So, within the framework of this article, no attempt will be made to constrain creative artists within a single definition or to catalogue their results.

The Mountains as Background

Bredt wrote with reference only to Europe: 'The last creative task embarked on in the Middle Ages was the representation of landscape, and the last aspect of that was the landscape of the Alps . . . the first appearance of the mountain scene in a work of art was not till the fourteenth century.'

In Europe it began with the great Italian painters of the day, such as Duccio and Giotto; they were followed in the next century by Pisanello, Bellini, Mantegna and Raphael. The painters of Umbria and North Italy knew the hillocks, ranges and rock-outcrops of their homeland very well; they used them mainly as backgrounds, limits, high features, to enliven glimpses between columns and through windows. Landscape seemed of value to them only as a contrast to religious scenes or architectural features.

It seems odd that even the artists who lived in the plains, far from the Alps, like the Netherland painters Jan van Eyck and Memling, resorted to mountains for romantic contrasts. It was much more natural that the Swiss, the Austrians and the Germans, just to the north of the Alps, approached their landscape painting problems in a more realistic way and brought mountains more into the middle ground of their pictures.

In 1444 Konrad Witz of Rottweil painted his lovely Basel altarpiece depicting Christ walking on the water, which he transplanted to the shores of Lake Geneva. Above the red cloak of Christ moving on the water rise the olive-green hills, with the Salève and Mont Blanc towering into a pale sky. Michael Pacher of Bruneck in the Pustertal, equally prominent as painter and wood-carver, who was dubbed 'the greatest German painter before Dürer', used the same approach. Into the panel depicting the building of the Church in his famous picture, completed in 1481, which decorates the altar at St Wolfgang, he painted a landscape of the Abersee in the Salzkammergut. Albrecht Altdorfer (1480–1538) of Ratisbon, was known as the 'artist of the true German Alpine scene'. The cosmic motion of the sky above lakes and mountains, the eruption of the sun above the horizon in his *Battle of the Issus*, are magnificent. His colours glow and blaze. Hills, rocks and trees are depicted to the life; there is hardly a picture or woodcut of his in which they fail to appear. He was the great master of the Danubian school.

Alongside him—beside Jörg Breu and Lucas Cranach—there was Wolf Huber, born at Feldkirch in 1490. In his masterly drawings, we can recognize scenes in the Vorarlberg, the Grisons and the Salzkammergut. In his *Lamentation*, dated 1521, there is a marvellously beautiful background landscape of a lake and hills.

The Swiss painter Hans Leu (1490–1531), whose *Orpheus and the Beasts* has an imposing mountain at its centre, painted in the same *genre*. Niklaus Manuel, surnamed 'Deutsch' (1484–1530) was of Italian descent, but settled in Bern. His colours are magical: in his picture *Pyramus and Thisbe*, the mountains go skywards in a wonderful sweep of deep blue.

There were two planets swimming in the skies of art in those days, Leonardo da Vinci and Titian. The latter, born at Pieve di Cadore in 1477, was a true son of the Dolomites. This outstanding master of the Venetian school could have been a great mountain painter, but he remained within the confines of the artistic ideals of his day and painted his saints and heroes in the foreground of distant mountain scenes. On woodcuts and engravings made from his pictures the craggy shapes of his homeland are more clearly revealed. Christoffel writes: 'The force and the deep understanding with which Titian portrayed the character of mountains is amazing'. I should like to apply his words to the other great painter of the day, Leonardo da Vinci (1452–1519). This Florentine—the true genius of the Renaissance—was also a mountaineer. According to alpine histories he climbed an 8,000-foot peak in the Monte Rosa group in 1511. His marvellous drawing, *Great Alpine Landscape in a Storm*, is executed from his favourite bird's-eye view. Even in his most glorious pictures, the St Jerome, St Anne and the Mona Lisa, the distant blue range of lofty peaks is always in evidence.

Albrecht Dürer (1471–1528), a German who lived north of the Alps, is rated as the pioneer of alpine landscape-painting. After studying with Michel Wohlgemuth at Nuremberg, he went on his travels. At Colmar he met Martin Schongauer. During their journey to Venice, he met at first-hand the Alps and Mantegna's paintings. In 1506–7 he spent another year in Venice, but we find representations of alpine scenes in his works as early as 1494. He sketched the mountains, the structure of their rocks and their perspectives with the same virtuosity he exhibited in his renderings of hands, hair and grasses. The observation and reproduction were as exact as his imaginative and powerful breadth of application.

In his engraving *Nemesis*, one can recognize in reverse Klausen and the Monastery of Säben in South Tyrol. Many of his woodcuts, of which an impressive example is *The Visitation*, include alpine details. If one compares Dürer's woodcuts, for example, with the stylized, ill-proportioned illustrations in Hartmann Schedel's *Liber Chronicarum* (1493), one is instantly impressed with Dürer's superiority in the painting of mountains, though Bredt is perhaps exaggerating when he writes: 'He was a greater pioneer than Leonardo da Vinci himself.' Naturally, Dürer's influence on the future representation of scenery was great. Yet, with the exception of Altdorfer and Huber alone—landscape remained as a background feature of paintings.

Hans Burgkmair of Augsburg, Hans Schäuffelein of Nördlingen and Leonhard Beck are worthy of mention, not for their artistic skill, but for their detailed representation of mountain features and the events experienced in the mountain setting. The Emperor Maximilian I (1459–1519) was the patron who commissioned their work. Dürer had illustrated the royal prayer-book. Of the Emperor's planned list of books, only the

Theuerdank came to fruition. Between 1517 and 1679 this book, illustrated by more than a hundred woodcuts, appeared in six editions. The three artists named above were commissioned to do the drawings. Jost de Negker is said to have done the woodcuts from them. They constitute the first representations of alpine dangers and alpine techniques.

The Netherland painters of the late Middle Ages devoted themselves, with all the aids of light and shade, to the realities of life. For them the worldly aspect no longer held any taboos. The picture of mode and custom ousted the mythological story. Clear-eyed and with the lowlander's nostalgic pleasure, they saw the whole lively mountain-scene, from its tufts of grass, its blossom-laden branches to the towering stature of its peaks, as a single entity. But they resolutely kept them at a respectful distance from their homeland on the canvases they painted.

There is Pieter Brueghel the Elder, for instance. Once denigrated as a peasant-painter, he is also known as the first modern master of landscape. He took countless compatriot painters with him through Switzerland to Italy as a young man. Karel von Mander commented: 'Brueghel on his travels drew so many views from nature that he swallowed all the mountains and rocks, only to spew them out again when he got home.' Brueghel's views of natural scenery and cities found wide acceptance as engravings, made and published by Hieronymus Cock.

It was only in his later years that Brueghel showed himself as a pioneer of landscape-painting. In his *Winter scene with returning hunters* and *River scene with farmers sowing*, the painting of the hills is wonderful. For him the scenery no longer constituted a background, but the true world in which life goes on. His men and his hills were in accurate proportion. Lucas van Valckenborch, Jodocus de Momper, Paul Bril, Roeland Roghman and the very individual Hercules Seghers continued along the road Brueghel had opened up.

The Mastery of Landscape-painting

The sixteenth century ushered in the first scientific exploration of the Alps. Conrad Gesner, the 'German Pliny', published his three-volume *Tierbuch* (Book of Animals). Ägidius Tschudi (1505–72) became the first alpine topographer. In his *De Alpibus Commentarius* (1574), Josias Simler produced the first monograph on the Alps. These books all contained a wealth of woodcuts.

At about the same time as Columbus was bringing back news of a New World, a doctor in Zürich, Konrad Türst, at the heart of Switzerland's narrow mountain confines, drew the first naïve map of the Alps. In his map of Central Switzerland (1538) the mountains are presented as a huddle of similarly-shaped cones, an 'ant-hill' method of presentation, which was to endure for 250 years. Others, like Burgklehner and Apian, gave a bird's-eye picture of the mountains, planting trees among them and showing chamois jumping on the ridges.

All the same, there was a noteworthy effort on the part of the topographers to provide an accurate and realistic picture of the Alps, on maps and in engravings alike. In their attempt to provide a real human need to see and learn a great many things, the works and atlases of the topographers corresponded to the periodicals and pictorials of later days.

Matthäus Merian the Elder (1593–1650) of Basel wrote sixteen topographical books of great value. In particular, his *Topographia Helvetiae* is rich in mountain pictures, greatly exaggerated, as for example in his representations of the rock-structures of Glarus and the Glärnisch. This was simply a sign of the times. The earlier Flemish painters had exhibited this same tendency to exaggerate, by making quite modest rocks assume alpine proportions, allowing them to go towering to the sky.

Merian was a restless creature. His unquenchable zeal for topographical undertakings led him to continuous journeying and activity, although in his own workshop at home he organized a method of producing pictures almost on the lines of a factory. He was also a

Eine andere Gefährligkeit/ darein Fürwitz den Edlen Theurdanck führt/ auf einer Gemsen Jagt.

IN Oesterreich ob der Ens/ kam Er abermahls in einem Gemsen steigen in Gefahr/ von wegen deß Schnees/ so sich zwischen den Fuß-Eysen geballet hatte/ also/ daß Er sich nirgend anhalten könte/ und gar nahe zu todt gefallen wäre; Aber GOtt half Ihme wieder glücklich darvon.

Wie Fürwitz den Edlen Theurdanck auf ein Gemsen Jagt führen liesse.

IM Halber Thal/ auf einer Gemsen Jagt/ ist Ihme begegnet / daß Er mit einem seiner Fuß-Eisen bestecken bliebe / und da man Ihme nicht zuhülff kommen wäre/ und außgelößt/ hätte Er Jämmerlich daselbsten verderben müssen.

Wie der Edel Theurdanck/ durch Anweisung deß falschen Unfalls auf einer Gemsen-Jagd/ abermahl eine Gefährligkeit überstund/ dann Ihm ein Stein seinen Hut vom Haupt schlug.

IM Steinacher-Thal jaget Maximilianus abermahl Gemsen/ als Er nun durch die Wände gieng/ wird ein Gerrassel über Ihme / und fällt ein grosser Stein auff Ihne/ daß Er buckend auff das Angesicht fiel / darnach sprang der Stein über Ihme auß / und stracks vor Ihme nider.

Wie Unfall Theurdanck in eine andere Gefährlichkeit führet/ under Schnee-Ballen.

IM Haller-Thal am Yn-Fluß/ als Maximilianus nach Wildprät zu Wald ritte/ begab es sich / daß sich drey grosse Schnee-Lainden von oben ablöseten / und als Berge auf Ihne herab schossen/ da Er aber das Gepolder hörete/ hat Er sich mit Zuruckzauffen deß Pferds/ von solcher Gefahr errettet.

Emperor Maximilian I's adventures in the mountains. Four woodcuts from *Theuerdank*, published in 1517.

keen illustrator of books: the Bible (1625–7), the *Gottfriedsche Chronik* (1630) and *Theatrum Europaeum*.

Landscape-painting, with its changes of mood and conditions, continued to develop. Prominent contributors to its successful evolution were Adam Elsheimer (1578–1610) of Frankfurt, the Dutch master Jacob van Ruisdael (1628–82) and from Lorraine, Claude. They painted skies, clouds, showers and the wide-open spaces in fine tones and with fine understanding, giving fresh impulse to the painters who followed them. Mountains, however, had still to be discovered afresh as subjects for canvases. During the seventeenth century their steep, savage shapes seemed to disturb the harmony sought after by the artists of the day. At the beginning of the eighteenth century nature had to give way to theatrical unreality.

Rome was a magnet that drew all European artists irresistibly. They painted idyllic Italian landscapes, considering the rough alpine regions barbaric. A fresh impulse was wanted, and it came from science. In the first decade of the eighteenth century, Johann Jakob Scheuchzer of Zürich had his *Itinera per Helvetiae alpinas regiones* printed. In 1732 there appeared as the results of a five-weeks' tour through the Alps a poem, 'Die Alpen' by Albrecht von Haller, the most important naturalist of the time. It ran through thirty editions. Next came Jean Jacques Rousseau with his slogan 'Back to nature!' Suddenly the Alps had arrived in the drawing-rooms of the modish, bewigged society. J. L. Aberli, David Herrliberger, Gabriel Lory, Christian von Mechel, Johann Caspar Wolf and Adrian Zingg sought out the beauty-spots and made numerous engravings on copper, some coloured, of the alpine regions. These became the fashionable decorations for the walls of salons and ordinary living-rooms until lithography (1796) and steel-engraving (1820) were discovered as new processes of reproduction.

Rousseau had been a powerful force in attracting foreign tourist-traffic to Switzerland. A passion for nature and for shepherds' idylls became the fashion throughout Europe. To the pampered townsmen the simple life of the alpine peasants seemed a stimulating change.

Mont Blanc, the highest peak in the Alps, was first climbed in 1786. To everyone's surprise the White Mountain, with its chaos of crevassed glaciers, became the water-colourists' pet model overnight. But they still saw their mountains as in a distorting-mirror: steeper, higher, more shattered and more terrifying than they really are. You only have to look at the painting of the Schreckhorn on p. 21 by Peter Birmann (1758–1844) to see a forest of rock spires rising above a shattered glacier. Small wonder: as late as 1755 Samuel Johnson had described mountains as diseased eruptions on the earth's surface.

The eighteenth century had devoted its efforts to documenting the Alps in miniatures; the copper-plate dominated. Few large paintings of purely alpine landscape were produced. The main patronage still came from the ecclesiastical-feudal upper stratum, which commissioned and sustained artists. It was the nineteenth century which was at last to make up lost ground and fill many gaps in the art of landscape-painting—including the specialized field of mountain-portrayal.

Josef Anton Koch (1768–1839) set up a milestone on the road. He was a peasant lad from Obergiebeln in the Tyrolese Lechtal, who was to revive the 'heroic landscape'. The course of his life led southwards. Discontented, he left his school in Stuttgart. In 1792 as he made his way into Strassburg, still disturbed by the Revolution, by way of the Rhine bridge, he cut off the plait he had worn till then and sent it to his teachers. He then made his way through Basel and Switzerland to Italy, staying in Rome from 1795 to 1812, then spending three years in Vienna, and returning in 1815 to Rome, where he remained till his death.

His picture *The Schmadribach Falls*, painted in 1812, attracted great praise. It shows snow mountains capped by clouds, a foaming waterfall and the clear trickling of water over bare rock, separated from the foreground by a belt of brownish woodland. Back in Vienna he painted *The Bernese Oberland* from his sketches, and three copies of the picture followed.

Josef Anton Koch: The Bernese Oberland. This oil painting, which is now in the Vienna Gallery, was described by Bruno Grimschitz as 'an epic of the simple life, in a setting of nature at her grandest and loveliest'. Like Koch, many intellectuals and latter-day Rousseaus saw in the Alps the ideal landscape. The painter once said to a friend: 'Here the creative spirit can drink in every separate detail and can build for itself the Entirety, as a draught from a rain-shower under the sheet-lightning of the imagination that idealizes everything.'

Grimschitz wrote: 'His contribution was to raise landscape painting to a historically important level, the sphere of the natural-heroic.' Many of his pictures are signed 'Giuseppe Koch Tyrolese'.

Koch reached a far higher artistic level than his contemporaries, Dorner, Wagenbauer and Dillis. Ludwig Richter (1803–84) came from Dresden to work with Koch in Rome and his painting of the Watzmann showed his trend, at that time, towards realism, before he reverted to the idyllic. Caspar David Friedrich (1774–1840) spent most of his working life in Dresden. He visited the Riesengebirge, but never went to the Alps. In spite of this he left us two great mountain canvases, one of the Watzmann, one of Mont Blanc, done from contemporary engravings. According to A. Wagner, Friedrich, who pursued a lone course and signed none of his pictures, was a magnificent painter of romantic landscapes, who sought to capture nature in her every mood and was, moreover, the first ever to create an atmospherically faithful landscape. Friedrich, himself an idealist, wrote: 'A painter must not just paint what he sees before him, but what he sees with his inner eye.' He showed his realistic skill in painting, for example, light snow lying on the branches of fir-trees.

Twenty years later, the Viennese Ferdinand Waldmüller approached landscape-painting with a very different palette. In the Vienna woods, and round about the Dachstein and the Königssee, he painted unsentimental, faithful, lively pictures, capturing the sunlight on meadows and tree-tops with his golden-green colour. He surpassed the heroic idealism of Koch and Friedrich's fine-spun romanticism. His slogan was: 'Without nature there is no truth!' In the romantic camp and partially influenced by Friedrich were Carl Blechen (1798–1840) of Cottbus; the Saxon Carl Gustav Carus (1789–1869), the royal surgeon, who in 1831 published nine *Letters on the Art of Landscape-painting*; the Norwegian Johann Christian Clausen Dahl (1788–1857) who taught at the Dresden Academy; Carl Philipp Fohr (1795–1818) of Heidelberg, and the three Dessau brothers Olivier, of whom Ferdinand (1785–1841), strongly influenced by Koch, followed the old German school of art. Above all, he was passionately fond of the Salzburg landscape, and in 1823 his series of lithographs, *Seven Scenes Around Salzburg and Berchtesgaden*, appeared.

Carl Rottmann (1797–1850), who came from near Heidelberg, continued the exploitation of the romantic in landscape. He came to Munich in 1922, made copies of Koch's pictures and became a mountain-enthusiast. His *Eibsee* attracted great attention in 1825; his paintings *Kochelsee* and *The Hoher Göll from the Hintersee* followed. Rottmann took care of the shape and structure of his mountains, confining his attention to their real nature, and loved rich, strong colours. After 1835 he introduced a monumental element into his views, in his cycle of Greek landscapes. His brother Leopold (1812–81) did much to spread the taste for mountain landscapes with his coloured lithographs.

Fifty years ago, Alexandre Calame (1810–64) was held to be the greatest alpine painter of the nineteenth century. He concentrated exclusively on the painting of mountains, starting by colouring prints. By the time he was twenty-five he had started to paint large Swiss landscapes, whose cloudy skies were at times reminiscent of Ruisdael's colour-values. He was enthusiastic about Meuron's picture of the Eiger (1825), which shows that gigantic, icy tooth mirrored in a tarn. Calame's pictures aroused widespread notice: they were exhibited, and sold well. They were on show in Paris every year for so many years that they were jokingly referred to as 'Calamities'. Paul Ganz wrote of him: 'Alexandre Calame became the best-known painter of the Swiss alpine landscape'. Calame himself reproduced his entire output in his lithographic publications, and in 1844 he did the illustrations for Toepffer's *Voyages en Zig-zag*.

It is impossible to ignore the influence of English artists on mountain painting in the nineteenth century. The most important was J. M. W. Turner (1775–1851). He knew the Lake of Geneva, Mont Blanc and the Rigi and, in Hazlitt's words, painted pictures which reflected the very elements themselves of air, land and water. Turner, like Constable, who was a year his senior, was a strong opponent of the classical Dutch landscape school. Mathey wrote that Constable no longer showed any of the influence of Ruisdael or Claude, but painted his own reactions to the living nature he loved. He detested any 'museum atmosphere' and was the first to see things with the eye of an Impressionist.

J. R. Cozens (1752–99), a most important predecessor of Turner, painted large watercolours of alpine scenes, the best-known probably being that of the Chamonix Aiguilles and Mont Blanc. A lesser, but still famous, landscape artist was John Varley (1778–1842), who handled Welsh mountain scenes with great skill in watercolour. Constable's great contemporary, Richard Wilson (1714–82), though he never painted in the Alps, is famous for magnificent Welsh mountain paintings, particularly his *Mount Snowdon.* Elijah Walton the younger (1832–80) of Birmingham was the first artist to take advantage of the foundation of the Alpine Club and painted many alpine views. He was a forerunner of the far more important E. T. Compton.

The French, though leading the mainstream of art, never had a strong feeling for mountain-painting pure and simple; but the Austrians were hard at work in the Eastern Alps. The Carinthian painter Markus Pernhart painted a 50 × 8 foot panorama from the Gross Glockner. He climbed the mountain four times in 1857, three times in 1858 and twice in 1859 to compose his picture.

The Viennese Thomas Ender (1793–1875) became a professor at the Academy and a Court painter; he travelled to Brazil and South Russia and accompanied the Archduke Johann on his mountain travels. Friedrich Gauermann (1807–62) first learned painting from his father, studied later at the Academy in Vienna and was rated a good landscape painter. Rudolf von Alt (1812–1905) did much to revive the stature of the watercolour.

Albin Egger-Lienz (1868–1926) is known for only one mountain landscape as such, his *Mountain Scene*, painted in 1911; but his pictures of mountain peasants sowing and scything, eating their midday meal, at the font and at war are redolent of life in the alpine world. Many viewers were horrified by these coarse, craggy figures, his brash types and tones. But Egger-Lienz stood four-square to a cosy world, avid for refinement, to let them see what life really meant in the mountains—being born, fighting for life and dying. Egger-Lienz was born quite close to the home of Franz Defregger (1835–1921). Between 1884 and 1893 he pursued his studies in Munich near his famous compatriot and master; and at first his method of painting came under Defregger's influence. Later he followed his own individual forms and methods, to lift himself above the *genre*-painting of his time, above the scenes on alps, hunting subjects and the interiors of inns, the decorations of the worthy citizens' homes of the day, often painted with 'great feeling'.

Munich in the nineteenth century became a rendezvous and training-ground for landscape painters, with its Academy, the moors and lakes in the foothills, its mountain ranges and Föhn-clouds.

It was Johann Jakot Dorner (1741–1813) who instigated the first public exhibition in Munich in 1788. Among notable painters, Wilhelm von Kobell (1766–1855) came from Mannheim to settle in Munich in 1793 and his clean, cheerful pictures are still sought after today. Max Josef Wagenbauer (1774–1829), a Bavarian by birth, worked as a painter-geographer on illustrations of his homeland; the same applies to Georg von Dillis (1759–1841), a much better artist. Albert Zimmermann (1809–88) came from Zittau, fell under the influence of Rottmann and became the focal point of a school of landscape-painters, the 'Zimmerleute', a pun on his name, 'the Carpenters'. They preferred painting 'oak-trees in the wind' with a leavening of hills and a great deal of 'feeling'. Eduard Schleich (1812–74) and Adolf Lier (1826–88) raised the standard a little, both combining romanticism with realism. August Seidel (1812–88) went beyond what he took from Rottman, Schleich and

Lier; people praised him as the 'Bavarian Constable'. Many other names could be cited, but it was to be a long time before a true, powerful painter of mountains was to appear on the scene. The truth is that, in the 1870s, the standard of art in Munich was mediocre. Leibl, Trübner, Schuch and Theodor Alt all turned their backs on it: it was too difficult for a young talent to find a firm footing.

Such a talent appeared with Fritz Baer (1850–1919). The son of a high court judge, born in Munich, he gave up the law after passing the government examinations, and became a painter. He was fifty before he saw the high Alps in Switzerland. His first great Eiger pictures were met with acclaim in Munich, receiving the gold medal. More than any of his contemporaries, Baer realized the play of the clouds and the strength of the mountains. In his search for new methods of representation, he was forced by his temperament into the use of *impasto*, thereby achieving a dramatic, fluid style. In 1920 Uhde-Bernays wrote of him: 'This was an artist of great vision, who moved from Munich's ancient *palette* tradition to the very verges of Expressionism with swifter strides than the city-walls had ever seen before.' If, today, we search throughout the German-speaking countries for a talent standing in a similar relationship to space and its phenomena, with the same exciting approach and the same harmonious mastery of the fundamental formulae dictated by the use of colour, there is only one—Oskar Kokoschka.

The Final Heights

In the last quarter of the nineteenth century two great artists left their influence on mountain painting, Segantini and Hodler.

Giovanni Segantini (1858–99) was born at Arco near Lake Garda. His mother died young, his father emigrated, and Giovanni's boyhood was a hard one. He spent it in Milan, without a home, often without a meal, repeatedly striving for freedom while in houses of correction. Towards the end of the 'seventies he educated himself at evening-classes and eventually obtained a post as a drawing teacher. An art dealer bought his first still-life pictures for 30 lire. Married, he and his young wife moved out into the countryside, in the Brianza in 1881. His finest painting done there was *An der Barre*, showing a herd of cattle in front of cloud-covered mountains. He won his first gold medal with his *Last Hour of the Day*.

About his own methods he said: 'My chief aim was to trap the light, and I soon realized that if one mixed one's colours on the palette, neither light nor atmosphere resulted. So I found ways to arrange pure and clean colours by placing the colours I had formerly mixed on the paletta, directly on to the canvas, next to one another, and then left it to the retina of the eye to fuse them into their natural distance when the picture was looked at. In this way I achieved a certain fluidity of my media . . .'

In 1888 Segantini found his dreamland in the mountains of the Grisons, when he came to Savognin with his wife and four children and all of a shilling in his pocket. Here, however, he obtained 5,000 gold lire for one of his first pictures. The next two resting-places along his life's journey were Maloja and Soglio. In the Engadine he had at last found his true paradise. During the summer of 1899 he worked at his great triptych depicting Nature, called *Birth, Life and Death*. In September, when the days were growing chill, he was busy finishing the snowy range of mountains in the third panel, high up on the Schafberg, where he had built a hut to live in. While at work he was attacked by an inflammation of the appendix and he died of it. They had moved his bed close to the little slit of a window, and his last words were: '*Voglio vedere mie montagne*' ('Let me see my mountains').

Ferdinand Hodler (1853–1918), a Swiss, was born in Bern, like Segantini into a background of bitter penury. When he was fourteen, he was sent as a pupil to a 'vedute'-painter. In the summer of 1871 he came to Geneva. Dreaming of fame, he starved, slept in warehouses, painted shop-signs and views. His very first pictures showed the *chiaroscuro* of a

The Grivola, a watercolour by Elijah Walton (1832–80) for *Peaks and Valleys of the Alps*, London 1868. This English painter accused Turner of lack of strength in his mountain drawings, as well as exaggeration of their outlines. He himself was very active in the Alps, penetrating the loneliest valleys, seeing light and mist and the other effects as an artist, the mountains themselves as a climber. He was, indeed, as self-reliant and expert as the guide Ambrozio Dayne who in 1859, climbing solo, was the first to reach the Grivola's summit.

Rembrandt. As in the case of Segantini and Cézanne, they were born of admiration for great paintings of the past. In 1873 Hodler's *In the Forest* won him the Calame prize of 300 francs, but his work still met with lack of understanding. In the autumn of 1878 he went to Madrid. In 1888 Hodler reached a climax with his painting *The Avalanche*.

At the turn of the century his pictures of high mountains began to take pride of place in the general estimation of his output. Walter Hugelshofer wrote about them: 'This is a case of an artist finding a completely suitable subject for his art. Neither before nor since, except perhaps in Segantini's Engadine landscapes, has the grim, lonely world of the great peaks been expressed in painting with the same impressive power as in Hodler's. Yet he was a lowlander and never saw the mountains until he was a grown man.'

As incontrovertible proof of that judgment, his pictures of the Bernese Oberland and the Valais are there for all to see. The Lake of Geneva, too, was a subject to which he returned again and again; there, behind the pale-blue, serene lake and beyond an autumnal strip of brown countryside, rise the hills of Savoy and Mont Blanc. Even after he was stricken in 1917 by a mortal illness, he painted a dozen more views across his beloved lake, a broken man looking back from the threshold of eternity. He died at Geneva, aged sixty-five, on Whit Sunday 1918. The trees he had so often painted were in blossom.

Impressionism was a late development of naturalism: its main feature was no longer the object being painted in itself, but a free natural rendering (='impression') of the object in its full light-value. Corot's *Gust of Wind* blew effectively through the Paris salons. A recluse from southern France, Paul Cézanne (1839–1906), developed an entirely individual style. He painted the Montagne Sainte Victoire in so many different forms that it would be too much to include him among the great mountain painters, equally wrong to omit him. The cleansing of nature painting of its sentimental overtones went on. Matisse declared to Pissarro that an impressionist landscape must be 'a moment of nature captured in paint'.

In Germany, a forceful figure from East Prussia, Lovis Corinth (1858–1925), brought fresh accents into landscape painting. Starting out as an admirer of Böcklin, he developed into a dramatic innovator in the treatment of light, equally at home in Impressionism as, in his later years, in Expressionism. In about 1910 he came to the hills for the first time, and painted his first view of the Inn Valley, a panorama from the Klobenstein. In 1918 he built himself a house at Urfeld in Upper Bavaria, and his splendid series of Walchensee canvases followed. Living among them, he now achieved full understanding of the mountains.

In 1905 the German expressionists formed the circle in Dresden known as Die Brücke. One of it spiritual leaders was Ernst Ludwig Kirchner (1880–1938) of Aschaffenburg. He was both an idealist and an egocentric, suffered a nervous breakdown during the war, after which he moved to Switzerland for good. At Davos the mountains became part of his daily life. They had an exciting effect on this sensitive townsman and he painted them, like the painters of the past, in exaggerated shapes; his colours, however, came from a truly modern palette, producing a sharp subjectivity in his pictures. His Staffelalp pictures, painted round about the Sertigtal, were the result: *The Alpine Life* (1918), *Winter Full-moon* (1918), *Weinfluh and Schafgrind* (1920) and, in 1921, *Davos Under Snow*. He was also a powerful carver of woodcuts. But in 1938, depressed by the sequestration of 600 of his pictures in Germany, he committed suicide.

A member of the same circle was Erich Heckel, born at Döbeln in 1883. He was fundamentally a much greater lover of nature than Kirchner and travelled a great deal. His first visit to the mountains was in 1921; he came back again and again, to the Alps of Allgau and Berchtesgaden, to the Carnic Alps, the Oberland and the Engadine. He preferred watercolour to oils, and was also a master of the woodcut. His mountain scenes are painted in light tones, but are by no means pale. These pictures, done from memory (he never painted out of doors), he called generically 'Mountains' or 'Mountain Range'.

The Swiss, Ernst Hodel, who painted in Lucerne from 1908 onwards, was among the outstanding mountain painters of this century. Apart from his large murals, decorating such buildings as the Central Station in Lucerne, he painted beautiful and faithful mountain canvases, which are to be seen in the museums and art galleries of Geneva, Berne, Basel and Lucerne. There was also a Russian school which specialized in lighting effects on mountains and forests under snow—particularly sunrise and sunset 'glows' on the peaks—of whom the best were Gourmachev, Bessonov and Schultzé. Among present-day British alpine painters, Dr Howard Somervell, of Everest fame, is extremely competent in watercolours and oils, and the snow and mountain oil-paintings of E. Holroyd Pearce display a specially charming talent.

Probably the one name that stands out above all in contemporary mountain painting is Oskar Kokoschka, a native of Pöchlarn on the Danube, born in 1886. Strongly influenced at first by Romako and Hodler, in due course he came to fashion the essentially modern mountain portrait of our times. In 1910 Kokoschka painted *The Dent du Midi*; in 1913, returning from Italy by way of the Dolomites he produced *Tre Croci* entirely painted in green and blueish-grey. Even more powerful are *Mont Blanc*, rising above a vague indication of Chamonix, and his *Matterhorn* (1947), seen in a torment of the elements. Richard Scheid wrote of this picture: 'Kokoschka's mountains are always in geological convulsion; he knows that their aspect at any given time is only a split second in the earth's history.' His *Rhone Valley* (also 1947) is in a more friendly mood, while his *Delphi* (1956), a canvas of great breadth, depicts a monumental, transcendental nature enveloping man's little handiwork.

Franz Marc (1880–1916) took a stride forward towards the abstract painting Kokoschka carefully eschewed, and in so doing produced something definitely new. His picture *Tyrol* (1913) was described by H. K. Röthel as his greatest artistic achievement, showing 'his beloved mountain scene, transfigured by a vision of godlike qualities'.

Just as few sixteenth-century landscape artists could rival Altdorfer, so in our own time not every painter of mountains is a Corinth or a Kokoschka. Yet they have all had their share in discovering fresh traits in the countenance of the hills—the late-Impressionist Otto Pippel, the realists Curry, Bruno Flashar, E. von Handel-Mazzetti, Erwin Kettemann, Hans Maurus, Franz Schwetz and Robert Zinner; Karl Reiser, with his stark mountain modelling, Hans Herzing, with paintings of great peaks and cloud symphonies; the romantics, Edmund Steppes and Hugo Hodiener; the lyric painter of the Chiemsee, Rudolf Sieck; the water-colourists, Otto Kessler, Max Märtens and Wolf Röhricht, the suave Wolf Bloem and the disturbing Asmus Debus, Max Lacher, Anton Lamprecht and Thomas Niederreuther.

Painter-mountaineers

Alfred Steinitzer wrote: 'Before the Alps were first widely climbed, in about 1850, the Alpinists themselves were the leading illustrators. They were either first-rate artists with the pencil, as for instance Whymper and Payer, or the artists were first-class climbers like E. T. Compton, E. Platz and R. Reschreiter; or they had to become so, like McCormick, whom Conway taught to climb, so as to accompany him on his climbs and illustrate his books.'

The ideal, as the description denotes, were painters who also climbed well, as distinct from artists whose attitudes to mountains were purely platonic. Such men paint from fully-realized knowledge and experience, not from a mere passing contact and distant observation. For the most part they produce portraits of their mountains showing every fold and wrinkle. For the mountaineer wants to find his mountain pictures accurate, he wants to be climbing on real rock and ice, through his eyes. An art historian is often forced to adopt a different criterion.

The brothers Schlagintweit visited the mountains of Central Asia as long ago as 1854–58 and set a height record for that era with 22,250 feet on Abi Gamin. These tireless men brought back some 700 watercolours and drawings. The sketch *Traill's Pass with Nanda Devi Ghat* was painted at an altitude of 17,800 feet by brother Adolf (1829–57). This height-record for painting was only surpassed later by Reschreiter in the Andes and McCormick when he climbed with Conway.

Edward Whymper (1840–1910), who laid siege to the Matterhorn and succeeded in climbing it, to the astonishment of the alpine world, in 1865, was really the first to combine high mountaineering with pictorial reporting. A London publisher sent him to the Alps in 1860 with a commission to bring back sketches from mountain-climbs. Examples of the sketches he made while actively engaged on climbs appear in his books.

Most of these climber-painters were detailed draughtsmen, expert with the pencil before graduating to the brush. The unrivalled master in this field was Edward Theodore Compton (1849–1921), who was born in London. The family moved to Darmstadt when he was eighteen, and he made tours through the Odenwald and the Eifel. In Switzerland a year later he fell in love with the mountains and made up his mind to master the snow and ice of the high Alps in the cause of pictorial art.

What was the position of art in the Alps at that time? Josef Anton Koch had painted his idyllic landscapes, with their rainbows and waterfalls, during the first years of the nineteenth century. About 1830 a one-eyed youngster in Geneva set out to document the mountains in his paintings. This was Alexandre Calame. But in the Paris and Geneva salons the critics complained that it was all too naturalistic and lacking in poetry; his pictures were too much like Daguerrotypes; to produce artistic truth, one had to tell a few white lies about nature. Calame had painted his fifth version of *Monte Rosa at Sunset* before Compton was born. A year after that event, the death occurred in Munich of Karl Rottmann whose *Eibsee* picture had in 1825 breached the world of mountain- or rather foothill-painting, with its smooth, pleasant façade. There was undoubtedly talent in the Munich school, but nobody decided to follow Compton up into the great mountain ranges.

In 1872 Compton drew his first alpine sketch in the Valais, in 1879 his famous *Devil's Gorge* was hung in the International Exhibition at Munich and in 1906 the Prince Regent bought his painting *The Aiguille d'Argentière*. Even if he was at first not free from mannerisms and inclined to over-decoration of his foregrounds with figures, even if later on he painted the green meadows and forests much as his predecessors had done, he finally established himself among the solitude of the glaciers and peaks as the sole and indisputable master. He had the gift of capturing the atmosphere, the contours and the depths of the mountain scene, which he heightened by his handling of mist- and cloud-veils. In addition he commanded a marvellous and unique faithfulness to reality, achieved without any over-elaboration of detail. He produced a vast multitude of illustrations for books and periodicals. Steinitzer wrote in 1913: 'No present-day climber or artist has done anywhere near as much as Compton to open up the Alps pictorially.'

The colour plates opposite and on p. 164 are from a book on Mont Blanc by W. Pitschner, published in Geneva in 1860. They are coloured lithographs by C. Ullrich, entitled respectively 'The Ice World of Mont Blanc' and 'The Summit Structure near the Mur de la Côte with the adjoining ice-masses in the early morning alpine glow'.

How painters 'saw' the peaks. Plate 189, showing Mount Sinai and the dance around the Golden Calf, taken from Hartmann Schedel's *World History* of 1493, illustrates how artists liked to portray mountains in the Middle Ages: as humps in the earth's surface and heaps of stone, relatively overshadowed in size by human beings.

Albrecht Dürer became one of the great pioneers of mountain painting, having studied the alpine scene carefully on his journeys to Venice. His drawing *An Alpine Pass* (in the Escurial, Plate 191) is dated 1494. In it the eye meets no imaginary landscape; there is no difficulty in establishing that Dürer drew his picture of the Brenner road near Klausen, where it skirts the River Eisack. We can see that the single-track carriageway is partly blasted out of the rock and protected by a wall on the precipice side. At the same time the drawing is a documentary on the highways of old.

Albrecht Altdorfer's etching *Alpine Landscape* (Plate 190, of about 1520) shows how much at home the artist was in the Alps. Everything, trees, houses, mountains, is seen in its true relationship. Altdorfer has rightly been called 'the artist who opened up the Alps'.

In 1552 a lowland painter, Pieter Brueghel, crossed the Alps on his way to Rome. He worked his impressions of that Alpine crossing into his picture, painted in 1567, *The Conversion of Paul*. In it we see a giddifying rock-path crossing a precipice high above gorges, the plain at the foot of the mountains and beyond it the sea. Plate 188 is a detail from that picture. Brueghel actually crossed the Alps by Mont Cenis, a pass far from being as horrific as the one shown in his painting. It may be thought that it speaks for the experiences related to him by other travellers through the Alps as well as for his own. More likely still, the painter, inspired by his own past adventure, was trying to represent the frightening, hostile 'wilderness' of the mountain world in contrast to the plains and the sea-coast where people could dwell safely.

189

◀ 188

190

191

Old maps of mountain regions (Plate 192 is a section of a Swiss one by Matthias Seutter at the start of the 18th century) used to show the mountains as rows and rows of ant-hills. These humps are mostly nameless, for the whole of Western literature mentions only 47 summits known by specific names before 1600. They all look very steep and very high, but we should not suppose that they really looked so disproportionately high to the cartographers of the day. They probably used an accepted, if not intentional, exaggeration of the altitudes involved, much in the same way as the makers of modern relief-maps exaggerate the vertical by anything up to ten times of the horizontal, for greater ease of viewing.

Plate 194 (a detail from an illustration from the so-called *Schwazer Bergwerksbuch* published in 1556) shows what the famous town of Kitzbühel looked like in the mid-16th century. Plate 193, an engraving by Friedrich Bernhard Werner, portrays Salzburg at the beginning of the 18th century.

SALISBURGUM Saltzbürg
1 Castellu primariu Salisburgu arcolsum.
2. Orphanotropheum.
3. Suburbiu Saxu s. Stein.
4. Porta vallis Monialium.
5. Templum Cajetanorum.
6. Coenob. Monialium, Mons Monialiu dictum.
7. Portula S. Michaelis.
8. Nova Structura Principis et Symphonia campanaru.
9. Archi Episcop. Templ. cathedr.
10. P.P. Benedictini ad S. Petrum.
11. Templu P.P. Franciscanoru.
12. Residentia Archi Episcop.
13. Bracteariioru port. aquaria.
14. Coenob. P.P. Capucinorum.
15. Curia.
16. Arx Edmundi.
17. Templum Universitatis.
18. Magnu Theatru in aula Academica.
19. Hospitale Civicu ad Spir. S.
20. Vetg Turnis, Porta aquar.
21. Monial. Ursul. ad S. Marcu.
22. Mons Monachorum.
23. Novg aditus ad istum.
24 S. Iohan. magn. Hospitale.
25. Coenob. P.P. Augustinianoru in Suburbio molarum.
26. Ad S.S. Trinitate, Alumnau et Colleg. Virgilianum.
27. S. Sebastian Domg Fratrum et magnum Coemeterium, in quo Theophrasti Paracelsi Sepulchrum.
28 Porta Linziana.
29 Palatiu Comitis Lodron.
30 Palatiu Recreationis Principis et Hortg Ital. Mirabella.
2. Das Waisen Haüß.
5. Cajetaner Kirch.
7. S. Michaels thörl.
9. Erzbischöfl. Dom Kirch.
10. Benedictiner zü S. Peter.
11. Franciscaner Kirch.
12. Die Erzbischöfl. Residentz.
14. Capuciner Closter.
15. Das Rath Haüß.
17. Universitaets Kirch.
18. Der grosse Theatrum in aula Academica.
22. Der Mönchs Berg.
23. Der neüe Paß aüf denselben.
28. Das Linzer Thor.
29. Gräfl. Lodronische Pallast.
30. Hochfürstlicher Lüst Pallast und Welscher Garten Mirabella.

193

◂ 192

194

Alpine painters. At the beginning of the 19th century a group of artists discovered the Austrian alpine scene around Salzburg. Plate 200 shows them on their 'painting-trip': the brothers Reinhold and J. C. Erhard, with Ernst Welker, as sketched by their travelling-companion Johann Adam Klein in 1818. Gustav Jahn (Plate 195 reproduces his portrait, painted by Ferdinand Andri) opened up many difficult alpine paths. Of his own pictures he said: 'I would sooner get less money for them, but that they should be bought by people who understand what I am trying to express.' Jahn was killed climbing and lies in the climbers' cemetery at Johnsbach. Giovanni Segantini (Plate 201 shows him painting in the open near the Maloja Pass in 1898) became the great propagandist for the Engadine with his paintings. He died up at 9,000 ft, while at work on a composition he called *Birth, life and death*. Ernst Platz (Plate 196) and E. T. Compton spent a lifetime drawing and painting mountains, and their works were a great contribution to the development of mountaineering. Plate 199 is an illustration by Compton for Emil Zsigmondy's book *Im Hochgebirge* ('Among High Mountains'): it shows the snow-white Presanella and four tiny figures in a silent world of white.

Many artists painted the Alps because the eternal fascination of the mountains had gripped them. Examples are Erich Heckel born in Döbel on the Mulde in 1883 (Plate 197 is a self-portrait) and the Swiss painter Ferdinand Hodler, whose painting *The Wetterhorn* (Plate 198) dates from 1887.

195

196

197

198

199

200

201

The heroic and the sentimental. The mountain scene and the mountaineer's life were long regarded in these lights and this was duly reflected in art.

The Emperor Maximilian's adventure on the Martinswand had for centuries appealed to men's minds: the story of how he had lost his way on the face, the common folk praying for his safety at its foot, and then the arrival of the chamois-hunter (later in the legend transmogrified into an angel) in time to save him. The Romantic painter Moritz von Schwind enshrined the story in about 1840 in a painting (Plate 202) which resulted in a vogue for pictures of lost climbers being rescued by angels or mysterious mountaineers. L. Bode called his etching of 1864 (Plate 203) *The Alpine Bride*, while in Plate 204, E. T. Compton portrays a kindly fairy of the Alps floating through the sky.

When in 1887 Eugen Guido Lammer, a contemporary of Nietzsche's, made his attempt on the west face of the Matterhorn, he wrote that he suffered from 'an unquenchable thirst for fatal dangers'. An avalanche which precipitated him and his companions 700 ft down the mountain quenched that thirst for a while. Ernst Platz's painting *Death and the Climber* (Plate 205) is an historic document of the period when it was painted: many climbers felt that way about their mountains. Indeed, Plate 206, a painting by Erwin Merlet, entitled *A Nasty Moment*, shows how long that sentiment endured, for it was painted in 1920. Merlet was one of the first to attempt the famous, even notorious, Schleierkante (the Arête of the Veils) in the Dolomites.

203

204

 202

205

206

Artistic licence. Matthias Merian's *Topography of Switzerland* appeared in 1642, and included a view of Glarus (Plate 208). In 1933, three hundred years later, Ernst Ludwig Kirchner made his woodcut *Mountain scene near Glarus* (Plate 207). Neither representation corresponds with actuality, and yet they are acceptable and recognizable portrayals of this corner of Switzerland.

Plate 209 is a 19th-century picture of the Matterhorn. In 1947 Oskar Kokoschka painted the mountain as no less excessively steep and sharp (Plate 210). But that is how the Matterhorn strikes every beholder; only photographs reveal its ridges to be less steep. The artist claims the liberty to reproduce things as he sees them. The young painter Ludwig Richter once wrote in his diary: 'Those who imitate nature slavishly will always produce the least natural result, just because they miss the over-all effect.'

207

208

209

210

Petit Mulet
Petit Mulet
Mur de la Côte

He was tireless both as a climber and as a painter; Karl Blodig, some ten years younger, who climbed every 'Four Thousander' in the Alps, testifies to this. When his companions rested, Compton sketched. He brought home crammed sketch-books from the Eastern and Western Alps, from Corsica and the Lofoten Islands, from the High Tatra, the Balearics and the North Cape. When he was 70, he was still fit enough to enjoy a sunset on the summit of the Gross Glockner. When he died in March 1921, the colours on his last painting had not yet hardened in his studio at Feldafing on the Starnberger See. At his testamentary request his ashes were committed to earth near the Zugspitze. He will always attract the admiration of mountaineers as an artist and technician who never falsified nature. His forty-year-old son, Harrison Compton, took over his father's easel, determined to carry on that great artist's tradition in the same spirit.

Younger than Compton, but a no less devoted mountaineer was Ernst Platz (1867–1940). The son of a professor, born at Karlsruhe, he went to study in Munich. After his *Memento Mori* he painted the first German climbing picture in 1894, portraying a climber on steep rock. Platz was much sought after as an alpine illustrator, even if his representation of figures may seem a little old-fashioned today. His mountain pictures are clear and clean, and free from any straining after effect, though perhaps a little dry. His animal-studies are masterly, his portraits, as for instance that of the old Ramsau guide Kederbacher, true to the life. He was eighteen when he climbed his first 10,000-foot peak. In his climbing-diary there is the entry of the first guideless climb of the east face of the Watzmann. In 1898 he accompanied Dr Hans Meyer to Kilimanjaro; in 1903 and 1911 he visited the Caucasus. He climbed and painted the great peaks of the Alps, the Dent Blanche, the Matterhorn, Piz Bernina; he loved the Karwendel, and later in life spent much time in the Arlberg.

Rudolf Reschreiter (1867–1938) also attended the Munich Academy, after completing his studies in Law, preferring a painter's life. He made accurate panoramic drawings, as for Heinrich Schwaiger's guide-books to the Wetterstein and Kaisergebirge. His pictures exhibit a meticulous reproduction of all natural features, somewhat at the expense of general artistic merit. His numerous pictures in tempera mostly depict a grayish violet sheen on snow and rock. In 1903 he accompanied Dr Meyer to the Ecuadorian Andes, climbed Chimborazo and Cotopaxi and brought home more than 100 pictures.

Of exactly similar age was Zeno Diemer, who painted the sea and the hills. It was not till 1884 that the support of patrons enabled him to go to the Munich Academy, where he was later to become a professor. Oberammergau became his second home. After journeys to the Far East and North, he sought to portray the beauty of the sea and of the hills in naturalistic watercolours and oil-paintings. He climbed many peaks and was in fact the first climber to reach the left-hand Fernerkogel in the Ötztal Alps.

Hans Beat Wieland was a better artist. A Swiss, coming from St Gallen to Munich, he soon parted ways with the 'inspired romantic-idealism' of the Academy. So he turned to the mountains themselves for instruction. Henry Hoek wrote of him: 'The basic quality of Wieland's mountain paintings is the unsparing honesty they exhibit both as pictures and as representations of the object painted.' As early as 1896 he devoted himself whole-heartedly to skiing.

Gustav Jahn (1879–1919) studied at the Vienna Academy and gave half his short life to climbing and painting mountains. The colours of his pictures are subdued and astringent, his Dolomite rocks glow reddish, and larches cover the slopes in raiment of autumn gold, like torches. In one of his last canvases, *The Pelmo*, he left two-thirds to a magnificent sky. He was one of the best climbers of his day. Among about twenty first ascents to his credit, we will only list the north faces of the Hochtor and Triglav in 1906 and of the Presanella in 1908. During the First World War he made first ascents in the Dolomites as a P.T. instructor. He fell to his death from the north arête of the Ödstein in 1919.

Adalbert Holzer, the Guglia di Brenta.

Jahn's Viennese friend Otto Barth (1876–1916) went his own way, painting figures and landscapes unmistakably his. He did many illustrations for periodicals and books (e.g. *Gefahren der Alpen*). His best-known picture is *Morning Prayer on the Gross Glockner*, showing guides at prayer in the harsh light of dawn beneath the summit-cross. The use of colour and the light-effect remind one of Segantini. Although he had done many difficult climbs with his brother Hanns, and other Viennese climbers, including the north face of the Reichenstein with Gustav Jahn himself, he was forced to abandon the rope and ice-axe at an early age owing to heart-trouble.

Otto Bauriedl (1881–1961) studied under Franz Stick in Munich. In 1905 he did the controversial illustrations for Erich König's book *Empor* (Excelsior), then passed through the style of his early days and a 'blue period'. 'He was unique among German painters, a phenomenon who passed from a romantic approach to absorption with the problems of light, yet remained true to a lyrically sensitive rendering of the beauty of mountains,' wrote Anton Schmid. He often painted in a tent with the thermometer at twenty below zero and was a passionate devotee of solitary climbing, among his solo climbs being the east face of the Lamsenspitze; his finest achievement was with his painter friend Adalbert Holzer, when they made the first ascent of the Spritzkarspitze's north face in the summer of 1902.

Adalbert Holzer (1881–1966) was born in Munich on the last day of 1881. There he learned to paint on glass and attended the Academy. His real love was natural history, but as a painter he graduated from drawings and illustrations to watercolour and oils, from a romantic approach through a dry realism to a harmony of colour and form. After 1920 he spent many summers on a farm in Gramais and specialized in painting the Lechtal mountains. He continued to climb till late in life.

Otto Oppel (1881–1964) of Heidelberg came to art from making *objets d'art*. He drew and painted with a delicacy reminiscent of Japanese work. His most important climbs were the ledge which bears his name on the Predigtstuhl in the Wilden Kaiser, a north route on the Hochwanner and the West Buttress of the Langkofel.

Julius Engelhard (1883–1964) was born in Sumatra, came to Munich, where he studied under Franz von Stuck, painted powerful mountain pictures, drove racing cars and liked flying over the Alps. In his later years he turned Surrealist. A climber from his youth onwards, he preferred long ridge-climbs and difficult faces like the east face of the Trettachspitze.

Erwin Merlet of Meran was a doctor but temperamentally a painter. He went straight into the war from the Munich Academy of Art, joining the mountain-guide courses in the Grödner Dolomites, where he soon did some first ascents with Gustav Jahn. His finest climb was that of the Arête of the Veils on the Cima della Madonna with Gunther Langes in the summer of 1920. Memorable among his pictures are *Death, the Companion* (the same subject as Ernst Platz treated in his *Memento Mori*), his Dolomite paintings redolent of their atmosphere, and his free, individualistic pen and ink sketches. He died at Bozen when only thirty-five.

Egon Hofmann-Linz, too, lived his life for mountains. His pictures, which include woodcuts, exhibit a moderate form of Expressionism.

Gustl Kröner came from Traunstein. His pen and ink drawings and *pointilliste* oil-paintings showed great promise, but unfortunately he did not pursue his artistic leanings. In the mountains, he was an extremist, accomplishing the third ascent of the Sentinel Route on Mont Blanc, the Charmoz north face direct and the second ascent of the east face of the Watzmann in winter. In 1932 he visited the High Atlas, but was killed by a falling stone at the foot of the north face of the Matterhorn in the following year.

Georg Maier of Ulm was comparable with Kröner among modern climbers. For his black-and-white studies and oil-paintings he adopted large forms, and followed Purrmann's colouring and used heavy *impasto*. He was at home on the most difficult rock-climbs and did numerous important climbs in winter and on ice (the Walker Buttress of the Grandes Jorasses and the Brenva Face of Mont Blanc). In the summer of 1957 he was killed on the Wildspitze, when a cornice broke away.

Our world and our life have undergone immense changes in the space of two generations. So have art and pictures themselves. We denizens of this century have lived through the most headlong break-through experienced by any age. This again is reflected in art. The herald of change here was Vincent van Gogh, who broke into nature with his fierce, feverish restlessness. The Fauves—the 'Wild Men' of Paris—devoted themselves to the application of pure, unadulterated colour. The Expressionists registered their protest against the painting of nature in an elegant style. Cubism came to visualize a solution of the problem in geometric rules. The Surrealists moved into the realms of unreality and phantasy, and finally abstract art turned away from objectivity in any form. This, of course, ruled out mountains.

Fifteen years ago E. W. Bredt wrote: 'Every age has its own style. Artists of every era follow artistic stenograms their contemporaries are capable of understanding.'

One fact stands out. The artists of every age have left us a rich heritage. We have the drawings of Leonardo and Dürer, works of true genius, the glowing nature-paintings of Albrecht Altdorfer, the heroic landscapes of Josef Anton Koch, Ferdinand Waldmüller's canvases, full of the joy of life, and the colour-explosions of Lovis Corinth and Oskar Kokoschka.

And if, in days to come, a painter depicts the earth and the universe—black sky, stars and fire—from a space-capsule tearing through the void, or the sterile, barren wilderness of the moon, be sure that nature will make itself felt, and with it the mountains and their thousand faces. There is no atomic power capable of moving the mountains and, so long as man draws breath, he will be familiar with their stenogram, the upthrust of the vertical.

MOUNTAIN PHOTOGRAPHY AND FILMS

Karl Kolar

In the days of Ferdinand Georg Waldmüller (1793–1865) and Camille Corot (1796–1875), those two sensitive poets of the landscape, whose aims were truth to nature and clarity, came the discovery, between 1837 and 1839, of a new pictorial technique, the Daguerrotype. To match the ordinary man's growing freedom to travel, the spread of railways, the foundation of popular newspapers (the *New York Herald*, 1835) and the issue of Baedeker's *Handbook for Travellers Through Germany and the Austrian Empire*, a strong desire had arisen for a pictorial record which any layman could produce, using a technical apparatus.

Just at the time when Caspar David Friedrich (1774–1840) was painting landscapes, which in their inspired harmony and simplicity mirrored the longing for peace and quiet, for the solitude of high mountains and the sea-shore, for restfulness itself; at a time when Eichendorff wrote his romantic-poetic novel *The Life of a Good-for-nothing*, Joseph Nicéphore Niépce (1765–1833), an officer of the Revolution, descended from a family of Burgundy vintners, discovered a completely new approach to the 'art of light and shade'. Louis Jacques Mande Daguerre (1787–1851), a Parisian scene-painter, who had gone into partnership with him, succeeded in 'capturing the scenes offered by nature without the intervention of a draughtsman'. His invention was the process bearing his name, the Daguerrotype (1837).

The discovery of photography can be compared with that of printing with movable type. Its function is to reproduce the object photographed in all its exact reality: a photograph is the reflection of natural fact.

As early as 1840, the infant technique, only discovered a year or two before, was employed, 'by means of light-pictures . . . to capture a true representation of the marvellous ice-formations of alpine glaciers by the use of heliography'. One of the very first was a Daguerrotype made in 1846, showing the Rofner Ice-lake, far up in the Ventertal, among the Ötztal Alps, which had been created at an altitude of 7,300 feet by the rapid forward movement of the Vernagt Glacier. Its ice-masses had now dammed up a sheet of water, threatening all the hamlets down the long valley, in the event of a disastrous break-through. This interesting picture was reproduced in the 1949 *Handbuch für Gletscherkunde* (Handbook of Glaciology).

Shortly after 1850 a Frenchman, Edouard Denis Baldus, produced an early masterpiece of panoramic mountain photography, the view from the Mont Dore being reproduced in a 'light-picture' 50 inches in length. In the mid-nineteenth century there was a craze for alpine panoramas. About 1854 Friedrich Martens, from a level of 6,000 feet, made a Mont Blanc panorama, consisting of 14 sections. A contemporary description gives some idea of the sensation produced by this photograph: 'There can be nothing more marvellous or impressive than this panorama. There is no stone missing; not a single ice-block has escaped the artist's careful hand. Only a photograph could provide the means of capturing and preserving such an experience.'

Till mid-century the cameras used for photography were of cumbersome and unwieldy construction. They were really only suited for use in studios, where heavy 'tripods' could be applied and where long exposures brought the requisite sharpness to the images on fragile glass plates of great size. Out of doors and even more so when climbing a mountain, specially-engaged porters were essential for lugging up the mass of photographic equipment.

When in 1856 the Bisson brothers undertook a photographic expedition from Chamouny (as it was then called) to Mont Blanc, they used collodium plates 12½ × 15½ inches. An army of porters took the great clumsy cameras, as well as a tent, with complete equipment for a dark-room and its baths and dishes, on their backs. Sad to relate, the high-altitude photographers on that occasion suffered misfortune on the way down when, owing to a porter's carelessness, the heavy plate-container, with the pictures it had cost so much effort to obtain, was smashed to pieces. All the glass-negatives were lost. Auguste Bisson, however, the younger of the two brothers, was obsessed by the idea of penetrating the mysterious and marvellous world of the White Mountain. So in 1861 he mounted a fresh expedition to photograph the 15,782-foot summit. In his own words, 'It is no child's play to take pictures at that height above sea-level. The first thing we had to do was to put up a tent in which to prepare the plates.' On this climb he used giant plates of 16 × 20 inches, and this time he got them down to the valley undamaged. He had managed to take three pictures!

There is a report in the 1862 *Photographic Journal* on this memorable ascent, which was not only remarkable from the photographic angle.

'Early on the morning of 27 July, M. Bisson was in Chamonix at the foot of Mont Blanc. The weather was favourable and it was decided to start. The whole company of tourists who occupy Chamonix during the fine weather season, all the inhabitants of the little village, which seems to be alive for only six months of the year, were assembled in the square to support the intrepid photographer as he set out on his climb with his guide Auguste Balmat, a worthy descendant of the first man to stand on Mont Blanc's summit, and the 25 porters who were to take turns in carrying the dark-rooms, the tent, the mirror-glasses, the collodium and all the rest of it, and finally all the photographic equipment of the cameras themselves to the top (the baggage weighed several hundredweight).

'The little army was greeted by cannon-fire as it set out. As the echo ran from summit to summit its resonances seemed to impress on the party the length of their journey and to threaten their courage. By 9 p.m. they had reached the Grands Moulets, the first stage, beyond which M. Bisson had failed to get a year before. A Bengal fire was lit on top of the rocks.

'Here they took a few hours' rest, but were early awakened by the fearful wind, which blew with great fury. Balmat, inconsolable at this bad turn in the weather counselled a delayed start. Two hours later the wind dropped, the weather cleared and it was decided to move on. Carefully keeping a grip on one another, their lanterns in their hands, they started up the mountain again, reaching the Grand Plateau at about 6 a.m.

'Disdaining to halt, they soon reached the Petits Moulets; but hardly had the courageous little band reached this height when a fearsome storm arose. A veritable hurricane held them in fetters, carrying with it such a pother of snow that they were surrounded by darkness and only with the greatest difficulty achieved shelter of some kind. Meanwhile every man of them was overcome with sleep which, as everyone knows, is fatal in these regions. M. Bisson then asked Balmat whether the tent could be erected at this spot. The guide looked at him in amazement and said: "Do you not, then, want to see Chamonix again? We have only just enough time to get back, God willing, to the Grands Moulets, for here the avalanches will come hurtling down and the snow will not long leave us in safety." So they set out, feeling their way, sightless, attempting to retrace their footsteps, clinging to each other, for they could distinguish nothing two yards ahead of them. In this way they descended a slope of about 45° some 1,600 feet long. They no longer walked, but rather slid, more rapidly than they wished, till at last they came to the Grands Moulets, and so at last reached the place they had left in the early morning.

'When the wind dropped, they took counsel and then sent the sick back to Chamonix, with a request for a reinforcement of seven men. Waiting on the Grands Moulets was

An alpine photographer in the middle of the last century.

tedious, but about 9 p.m. they heard singing. It was the Chamonix reinforcement, full of cheer and high spirits, approaching. The rest of the evening was pleasantly spent, all being revitalized and greatly cheered.

'At about midnight the sky cleared completely, lit by a full moon. It was a glorious night, a beautiful picture to contemplate. So: off again! They reached the summit at about 8 a.m. (on 29 July).

'It was now that M. Bisson's task of taking photographs at 1,600 feet above sea-level began in earnest, for such pictures do not take themselves. First of all, he had to put up the tent, under which, protected from the light, he had to pour collodium on the plates, with hands that must not tremble either from cold or weariness, and sensitize them in silver-baths. To make things harder, an irresistible desire to sleep overcame everyone. Nobody could or would move from where he then was. However, Bisson and Balmat, left entirely on their own, unpacked and assembled the equipment. The tent and the dark-room were erected, the glass plates sensitized, the lens fitted, and the prospect photographed. And what a prospect! Now it was time to process the picture, but there was no water in which to wash the plate. They had reckoned on melting snow with a lamp, but the flame, transported to so foreign a country, refused to burn in such rarefied air. . . . They detailed a man to keep the flame alive, but he fell asleep. A second, sent to relieve him, did likewise. In the end Bisson himself succeeded in producing some of this precious water. He ran to the tent, where only Balmat was on his feet, determined to see his task through.

'After two hours Bisson started all over again, determined not to go down without three negatives. And he got them, two good ones, one passable. Then he packed all his belongings single-handed, shook himself, woke everyone else up and started down to the Grands Moulets. There, anxious as he was to get back to Chamonix, he stopped again to take more pictures.'

Ernest Lacan described these pictures in the 1862 number of the *Photographischer Archiv.* 'In these pictures,' he wrote, 'the dangers to which the photographer and his party were exposed among the ice-fields are clearly revealed. In one picture they are seen moving over the perilous high levels, roped to one another, on snow which deceptively covers abysses; in another, we see them climbing steep summits, in which they hack steps to enable them to ascend. We are thus enabled to form an idea of the energy, the steely nerve and the will-power this courageous party needed to make the ascent. The magnificence of the contours, the splendour of these regions, the impressive effects of light and shade engendered by the sunlight on these mountains of snow and ice all go to make a wonderfully beautiful picture.'

The Austrian Alpine Association encouraged the art of 'light-pictures' from its foundation in 1862 onwards. In 1863, a studio photographer undertook a journey into the Glockner area, subsidized by the newly-formed Association, whose headquarters were in Vienna. The expedition, whose artistic director was the landscape-painter Adolf Obermüller, returned with a rich 'bag' of 91 good photographs. However, it seems that the break-through into the 'Optical Age' had not yet been achieved; for there turned out to be very few purchasers of these hard-won treasures. Led by Paul Grohmann, the great explorer of the Dolomites, an alpine detachment, 22 strong, of this first photographic venture climbed the 12,461-foot summit of the Gross Glockner on 4 August 1863, starting from the Leiter Hut and accompanied by the Vicar of Heiligenblut. Guides, photographers and porters climbed through the night by torchlight to the Adlersruhe, where they erected a black oilcloth tent covering an area 60 feet square. Through a circular aperture, one of the photographers watched and photographed the party as it went on. He used the figures of the climbers as a foreground to indicate the vast scale of the scene.

The 1864 *Archiv* reported as follows: 'The expedition left Vienna on 2 July 1863. Its main objective was the whole Tauern Range and particularly the Glockner group. Work began at

A contemporary woodcut of Auguste Bisson's Mont Blanc climb in 1861.

Wildbad Gastein on 4 July. On the 22nd they succeeded in crossing the Pfandlscharte, reaching Heiligenblut after a march of eleven hours. On 2 August they finished photographing the Pasterze Glacier and equipped themselves at Heiligenblut for the climax to their labours, the photographing of Gross Glockner itself. They started packing the equipment on the morning of 3 August and at 11 a.m. twelve porters went ahead to the Leiterhütte carrying heavily-laden crates. At about 4 p.m. the main party, reinforced by five Glockner guides and the Vicar of Heiligenblut, followed. The hut had been chosen by the guides for the overnight base. There they spent the evening in redistributing and lightening the loads as far as possible. After a short rest the head-guide, Tausch Jörg, roused the party and by 11 p.m. everything was ready for the start. The approach to the great peak, a long march by moonlight and flaming torches, on the part of the 22-man cavalcade was indeed picturesque . . .

'A short rest was taken on the moraine of the Leiter Glacier and, as this was the last point where water was available, the small kegs provided for photographic purposes were filled. At about 6 a.m. the whole party reached the Aldersruhe, the last place where the photographic apparatus could be set up, some 1,000 feet below the summit. The morning was wonderful and everyone in the best of spirits; the only discomfort being the icy wind which made itself so keenly felt up there at 11,000 feet, that even at 7.30 a.m. the prepared plate froze in Herr Jägermaier's hands. The main body of photographers established itself there, at the Adlersruhe. Meanwhile the landscape-painter Obermüller with the Glockner guides and eight indispensable porters prepared for the ascent of the summit, so as to take pictures of the Glockner which would more exactly record the vast scale of the scene; and, in fact, in spite of the tiny relative size of the figures it is possible in the photograph to recognize the huge frame of Tausch Jörg. . . . The climbers, too, were quite able, even from the very top of the peak, to follow the activities of the photographers. The exposures were excellent and by ten o'clock Herr Obermüller and his party were back with the photographers at the Adlersruhe. By 8 p.m. everyone was safely back in Heiligenblut where they were welcomed by mortar-fire and all the festive ceremonies traditionally accorded to climbers of the Glockner. Though the climb was indescribably exhausting for the photographers encumbered by their equipment, their efforts were crowned by almost complete success. In this way the most laborious enterprise of the whole tour was successfully accomplished and a rich and comprehensive photographic booty, from the peaceful beauty of the valleys to the Glockner's icy crest, brought home.'

Photography grew more and more popular with mountaineers towards the end of the century, as the more tractable format of cameras made them more easily portable on difficult climbs. Alpine sketchers like Edward Whymper (1840–1910), Julius von Payer (1842–1915) and the painters of high mountain scenes like E. T. Compton (1849–1921), Ernst Platz (1867–1940), Otto Barth (1876–1916) and Gustav Jahn (1879–1919) seemingly lost their justification as exponents of the mountain scene. The great climbers were now either themselves photographers or, like Prince Luigi Amadeo di Savoia and D. W. Freshfield, took talented mountaineer-photographers—Vittorio Sella, for example—along with them.

In 1864 the Dornach photographer Braun, with a supporting team of fifteen, crossed the Strahleck in the Bernese Oberland. The results of this laborious, dangerous, three-day expedition were five successful plates.

Twenty years after the discovery of the 'light-picture', a Chamonix guide became an enthusiast for the new art. At Les Moussoux he established the first photographic laboratory in the Mont Blanc area. This pioneer of mountain photography, Joseph Tairraz by name, still had to put the sensitive coating on to his plates before he could make an exposure. His equipment was clumsy and heavy. Many tourists came to Tairraz' studio to have their pictures taken in climbing gear against the background of the White Mountain's tumbling glaciers. Among them were Prof. John Tyndall, the first man to climb the Weisshorn above Zermatt, a member of the Royal Society, who wrote the famous book *Glaciers of the Alps* (1860); and Edward Whymper, first up the Matterhorn and world-famous for his book *Climbs and Scrambles in the Alps, 1860 to 1869*. Unfortunately, Tairraz's glass-plate negatives, dating back to 1861, were destroyed when in 1921 an ice-lake in a glacier burst its containing walls, causing the Arve and Arveyron to rise so rapidly that the cellar-storerooms of the Tairraz photographic shop were flooded and the irreplaceable plates ruined. When Joseph died in 1902, one of his sons, Georges, took over the family business. His pictures rank with the best mountain photographs ever taken. To get the best results, he used glass plates 20 × 25 inches, and the appropriate lens alone weighed 15 lbs.

Before 1870 two Frenchmen had taken photographs in the mountains for scientific purposes in the service of natural history. Aimé Civiale and Edouard Denis Baldus wanted people to know what the views from mountain summits looked like. Civiale made panoramas from Mont Blanc, from the Monte Rosa massif, from Wengernalp, Piz Languard and Eggishorn. In all, he made 41 such panoramic views. His 'Swiss Panoramas' were among the first serviceable photographs to come (1857 to 1868) from the ranges of Switzerland. He went up to heights of 10,000 feet to get them. His baggage on such occasions weighed about five hundredweight and his 10½ × 13-inch camera had a 30-inch lens.

Jules Beck of Strassburg left the Bernese Section of the Swiss Alpine Club more than 400 large-plate photographs. In the 'sixties and 'seventies he spent much time in the Gotthard area, the Grisons and among the great peaks of the Valais. He used a 5 × 7-inch plate-camera and a 12-inch lens. Beck gives some idea of the difficulties the mountain-photographers of the day had to combat. He relates how, on a climb of the Wetterhorn, he had exposed his glass plate four minutes instead of two, having in his excitement misread his lighting-table and taken the reading for 'overcast' instead of for 'bright sunlight', which ruled at the time. When the plate was developed another phenomenon appeared on it: the contours of all the mountains were visible several times over on the plate. During the course of a four-minute exposure the rear leg of the heavy tripod had been forced backwards into the soft snow by the weight of the camera!

In the 'sixties too, Richard Issler, the Editor of the *Neue Deutsche Alpenzeitung*, was already producing alpine 'light-pictures' in his Vienna publishing-house Artaria. Some of his 20 × 32-inch pictures were: 'Cimon della Pala, 3186 m, Primiero Dolomites' and 'Dolomites of Ampezzo: Monte Zurlon (God's Finger) with the Sorapiss Glacier and the Pfalzgau Hut. Frontier ranges of Tyrol and Italy.' The Viennese firm, Blechinger, printed his pictures as heliogravures, some of which are still to be admired on the stairway of the Austria Hut on the south side of the Dachstein.

Professor Friedrich Simony (1813–96), a founder member on the first Committee of the Austrian Alpine Association, was a fine mountain photographer. He illustrated his famous work *The Dachstein Area: A Geographic Study* (Vienna, 1895) with many of his own splendid photographs. One of his friends was the poet Adalbert Stifter, whose masterly tale 'Bergkristall' (Mountain Crystal) was inspired by one of his visits to Simony in Hallstatt. Simony was the pattern for the hero of 'Nachsommer' (Late Summer) in which Stifter tells the story of Simony's research-work. Simony also left behind him numerous maps and drawings, including his well-known panorama from the Schafberg, above Salzburg. He captured the beauty of the mountain landscape with his pencil as well as through the lens of a camera. Even if his pictures often served geographic purposes, they were not mere factual representations, but reveal the magnificence of the mountain world. Dr Friedrich Morton, the Curator of the museum in Hallstatt, where a whole room is devoted to Simony, writes about this pioneer mountain-photographer's work:

'The Museum at Hallstatt exhibits a series of Simony's original photographs in 7×9-inch format. Though these were taken eight decades or more ago, they are as clean and clear as on the day they were exposed. Today's photographer, working with a miniature camera, probably fully automatic at that, and with miniature film weighing practically nothing, has no conception of the difficulties under which a Simony had to operate! The heavy glass plates had, after meticulous cleaning, to be coated with collodium, having a content of iodized salt, to produce the iodine sensitive to light. These had to be exposed while still wet and then immersed in a solution of acetic iron-sulphate, the process reducing the salic-acid silver on the exposed surfaces to metallic silver. The fixing was done with zinc-alkali solution.'

The very thin negatives were intensified with a citrate solution of pyrogallol-silver-nitrate. As soon as they were dry, the easily-damaged plates were lacquered. The very fine-grain process is still in use in the reproduction of photographs. As luck would have it, there was found in the loft of the one-time 'Alte Post' Inn, at which Simony often stayed, a small sealed case he had had sent him there from Vienna, but had for some reason never opened. In it was the whole chemical equipment necessary for the above processing. It is on show in the Hallstatt Museum among a selection of Simony's photographs. Obviously Simony could not carry the huge tripod-camera, the heavy plates and all the chemicals himself. For this he required two porters, who climbed almost every summit in the Dachstein range with him.

On 4 April 1876 Simony gave a lecture to the Photographic Society in Vienna on 'Landscape-photography, from its scientific aspect', which was subsequently published in Dr E. Hornig's *Photographic Correspondence*. To quote Simony: 'Landscape photography, in its scientific aspects, has a mission, understood by few and accorded far too little value even among scientists themselves. If asked to summarize in a few words that mission, as it appears to me at least, I would say: "The photographic and that is to say the completely truthful reproduction of nature . . . will be carried on with a view to revealing every phenomenon of the landscape worthy of scientific and educational interest . . . of service to future studies and research".'

In his article 'Landscape photographs as a pictorial factor in the scientific study of alpine knowledge' (*Deutsch-Osterreichischer Alpenverein Journal*, 1880) Simony suggested that it would be of great service to the Club to produce a photographic atlas of the Alps.

The Club's old Journals are a treasure-house of mountain photography. A host of somewhat static exposures give us a picture of the original alpine landscape, which is being continually eroded in our own day. In the 1880 number of the Journal, in which Simony wrote his reflections on landscape photography, no photographs were as yet actually reproduced. Instead we find nothing but drawings 'from a photograph', the beauty of which is none the less apparent when we look at the old originals. No reproductions appeared till 1881, the first to be printed being one of Simony's: 'The Thorstein from the Simony Saddle'. This was the start of the photographic era in the Alpine Association.

Vittorio Sella (1859–1943) usually took with him into the mountains several porters, humping his heavy cameras and 10 × 12 plates. His camera still had no instantaneous exposure. He juggled with the length of exposure by speed in removing and replacing the lens-cover. He was one of the first to realize the importance of the foreground of a picture, and the introduction of human figures into mountain scenes as foreground-contrast. About the turn of the century, photographic 'retouching' techniques, 'high-lighting' parts of the negative, introduced an artificial artistic disservice to landscape photography. Sella, too, worked up such dark-room effects; but he and other climber-photographers gave a wide berth to 'hand-coloured' prints, to the doughy effects of the Bromoil print, which tried to imitate Rembrandt, to mountain-portraits produced more by retouching than by photography. Sella frequently preferred big enlargements, which are more suitable for reproduction purposes and also have the advantage of accentuating the sky-raking quality of great peaks.

He was the son of the Italian Finance Minister Quintino Sella, who founded the Italian Alpine Club, and a cousin of the poet of the Matterhorn, Guido Rey. In 1882 he made the first winter-traverse of the Matterhorn from Breuil to Zermatt. In 1889 he went out to take pictures of the Caucasus, which had not previously been photographed. In 1897 he travelled with Luigi Amadeo, Duke of the Abruzzi, to Alaska, where they climbed Mt St Elias (19,516 feet), the second highest mountain in the USA. The book, *The Explorations of His Royal Highness, Prince Luigi Amadeo of Savoy, Duke of the Abruzzi, to Mt St Elias in Alaska, 1897*, was illustrated by Sella's photographs and contained a full report of this alpine-photographic expedition.

In 1906 Sella accompanied the Duke, who also used his pictures for other publications, to the African peaks of Ruwenzori. This was the first exploration of the Ruwenzori range, the 'Mountains of the Moon', in the heart of Africa, which rises on the borders of Uganda and the Congo. True, they are seldom visible and their summits difficult to attain; for they protect themselves against intruders by fogs and rainstorms often lasting several weeks at the foot of the range and, in the neighbourhood of the highest peaks, by masses of snow. The Duke had planned the expedition carefully with the help of an Italian admiral and other research-experts, and invited Sella, who had already won a reputation through his pictures, to go along as its photographer. They climbed the highest peak, Margherita (16,816 feet) and also the slightly lower Alexandra. The Duke again published a book about his expedition, richly illustrated with Sella's pictures, in 1909. The author of both these reports was Filippi, the scientific adviser to the expeditions. In 1909 Sella visited the Karakorum with the Duke and D. W. Freshfield, one of the great British climbers of the day, whose book *Italian Alps Sketches* (1875) is one of the most attractive in the whole of alpine literature. The main objective of the expedition which included, besides Sella, Filippi, three alpine guides and four porters all from Courmayeur, was the ascent of K2, the second highest peak in the world. After establishing that a mountain of such altitude can be climbed only if it is a snow-dome and does not consist of mixed ice and rock, as is K2, the expedition contented itself with the 25,092-foot Bride Peak as its objective. During their attempt on this peak they reached a height of 24,600 feet, the highest point reached by man up to that time. Filippi again produced the report, a *de luxe* publication. *La spedizione nel Karakoram e nell' Imalaia Occidentale 1909* was full of Sella's wonderful photographs. He had become the most famous mountain photographer of his day.

An alpine photographer at the turn of the century.

Dr Fritz Benesch (1868–1949), a lawyer in the service of the directorate of the National Railways, was one of the most talented and important photographers of the era before the Second World War. It was in 1899 that his luxury publication *Bergfahrten in den Grödner Dolomiten*, illustrated by his own photography, was issued by the Munich publishing-house F. Bruckmann. Benesch explained in his preface that this work was closely connected with the completion of the Langkofel Hut at that time under construction by the Vienna Academic Section of the D.Ö.A. (Deutsch-Österreichischer Alpenverein). Ever since the summer of 1893 he had championed the cause of the Langkofel area, so as to force the agreement of the Club's members to the building of the hut.

His alpine guide-books, too, for the local Viennese hills—the Schneeberg (1897), Rax (1894) and Schneealpe (1925)—were furnished with his own pictures. Not only did Benesch popularize and describe the Viennese hills; he also owned the greatest collection of photographs of the Eastern Alps then existing. He processed all his own pictures and used to tell how in his youth he had lugged his heavy 7×9-inch Goldmann plate-camera with him, even on difficult and dangerous rock-climbs. Later on, he took with him a porter he had first trained in servicing and handling the apparatus. Of the dangers of mountain photography on climbs, Benesch described them as greater than the normal ones to which ordinary climbers are exposed. 'Not only are the dangers the same,' he wrote, 'but concentration on the photographic aspect reduces the high degree of awareness which self-preservation definitely demands during a climb. Like the Edelweiss-hunter, who takes risks and easily forgets the dictates of caution, so does the climber-photographer. The most dangerous situations in my long career of high mountain climbing were, almost without exception, brought about by the photography.'

In his book about the Dolomites, there is a passage describing how Benesch climbed the Little Fermeda (9,184 feet), one of the lower peaks in the Geisler Group, to take pictures of climbers on the Fermeda Tower. He describes how he and his guide Pescosta climbed down its granite arête till it was still broad and roomy enough to set up the camera, before it became too steep:

'Pescosta safeguarded me on the rope from above while I clutched the camera which was securely fastened to its hood. In this way I reached a point about 300 feet away from the notorious slab, with a drop of about 1,200 into the abyss between me and it, and there I swung like a steeplejack between the twin towers of a church.

'It is rare for two summits of similar height to stand so close together. The tall, sharp shape of the Fermeda Tower, the awful drop below me, the uncomfortable aspect of the people climbing beyond it were as impressive and grand as anything on a mountain face. The Tower (9,407 feet) is the noblest and sharpest of all the needles in the Geisler Group. It soared like some giant's thumb, a thin sliver of rock, pointing to the sky.'

Benesch's dearest wish was to take a picture of the famous, almost vertical, slab on the Fermeda Tower, notorious in the climbing world, and he was prepared to go to any lengths to get it:

'In order to reduce the continual foreshortening I now needed a place further up, where I could take a more horizontal picture. The usual line up the 60° slab goes diagonally upwards to the left, but in company with my friend P., I now climbed straight upwards till the face became too smooth to offer a better stance. . . . There was no need to worry, for P., comfortably seated, threw me the end of the rope and I tied myself to it. The greatest danger was to my camera, which I was holding tight by its hood in case of emergency.

'It was a good thing that I had taken the safety precaution of roping up, for when, in the usual way, I bent the upper part of my body down under the head-cloth, so as to get a better idea of how the picture was shaping and a proper view of the reversed image on the ground-glass screen, I was suddenly overcome, owing to my cramped position, by a kind of giddiness, and lost my balance. . . . I staggered, but my companion simply drew the rope in taut, while I leaned back against the protecting cliff. Then I took a tentative look down the face, my heart beating so loudly that I could hear it.'

In 1913, 1914 and 1915 Benesch's first 'nature pictures in colour' appeared in the Club's Journal. With a true sense of colour-values he used the red of the autumn-tinted teees as an effective factor in his compositions.

He was the first ever to introduce a scale of difficulty for climbs. This 'Benesch Scale' went from 7 (easy) to 00 (exceptionally severe). As in Grohmann's case, a statue was erected to him during his life-time, when grateful Viennese climbers put up a life-size memorial monument to him near the Otto Refuge on the Rax. From his rich experience as a mountain photographer Benesch laid down essential general rules: 'The photographer of mountain scenes must accustom himself to memorizing the shapes of his mountains. In this way he will soonest learn how to select his subject from the unbounded landscape and to capture the most effective sector of it. The most important thing is observation; practice in "seeing a picture" is everything.'

So Benesch became the leading photographic virtuoso in Vienna before the First World War. Many a railway-station was decorated with his landscape photographs, mostly of mountains. As a writer, too, he did honour to the Alps, at that time far from fully documented, with a deep affection for the mountain scene:

'The glory of great peaks can only be properly revealed in the right lighting conditions. To see such a landscape at its true best, the sun must be behind one or, better still, slightly from one side. Lit from behind one, it displays its individual colouring to the best advantage and by slightly diagonal sunlight every detail of its relief. A photographer may delight in *contre jour* pictures, but high mountains demand the sun on their faces. Too little attention is given to this inescapable fact, and so, much pleasure is sacrificed by those who go abroad among the hills.'

This theory of photography is now considered old-fashioned, but its results were pictures of a beauty never since surpassed, even with the aid of modern lenses and fine-grain films and processing. When in 1935 Benesch's alpine picture-book *Zauber der Bergheimat* (The Magic of My Mountain Homeland) was published in Graz, it was a farewell hymn to a world fast disappearing, thanks to technical advances and mass-movements. 'On a clear day,' he wrote, 'the great peaks soar skywards in the sunlight, incomparably beautiful, huge, noble and lovely—a sight which often seems to transcend all earthly frontiers. Our delight in it is one of the highest, noblest and loveliest feelings granted us by life.'

The Swiss Alpine Club's Journal did not publish photographs as early as the Journals of the D.Ö.A. and the Alpine Club itself in London. Besides 'light-prints', as photographs were then called, these handsome volumes contained woodcuts, zinc-plates, autotypes and photogravures, all taken from photographs. The first actual photographs published in the S.A.C.'s Journal were those by A. Rzewuski ('The Verstanklahorn, 3301 m'), Jules Beck ('Winter scene in the Dammastock range') and Ph. Gosset ('The West End of the Märjelensee, with the Aletsch Glacier') in the 1887–88 issue. The 1889–90 issue contained the first photographs of mountains outside the Alps.

In the 1888–89 volume, there are photographs by a Swiss, Emil Huber (Uto Section of the S.A.C.), of 'The Western Ringelspitz Group' and 'Climbers on the Fleckistock', and in the following issue, 'The Kleine Oberalper, 3085 m.' After 1890 Huber worked with a 5 × 7-inch camera, which he modestly called his 'miniature'. In place of a tripod he used an ice-axe fitted with an attachment for the camera. And his celluloid plates required exposures of not more than one and a half to thirty seconds.

Emil Terschak (1858–1918) started by drawing technical climbing sketches of mainly exaggerated alpine scenes. After 1900 he took up alpine photography and became one of the first photographers to take good pictures of actual climbing scenes on steep rock. Before the 1914 War, a book of his, *Photography Among High Mountains, by the Experienced Climber and Photographer, Emil Terschak*, saw the light of day. In it are many 'useful hints, in word and picture, about the sort of situations met with by mountain photographers'.

Eduard Lankes, who founded and worked for the *Deutsche Alpenzeitung*, was one of the first who dared to take fine pictures of the moods of the mountains, showing the dream-like poetic aspects offered to the beholder. His picture 'Late Autumn' (1903) achieved effects produced till then only by artists with paintbrush or pencil.

Willi Rickmer-Rickmers (1873–1965), the founder of the Alpine Association's library in Munich and leader of its first expedition to the Pamirs in 1913, published splendid photographs of mountains far beyond the Alps.

The first photographs in the *Journal for Members of the Alpine Club* in Britain are to be found in Vol. X of the *Alpine Journal* for 1880–82. In a report on climbing ventures and scientific observations, W. F. Donkin shows a panorama of 'The Nadelgrat from the summit of the Dom'. And there is a lithographic reproduction of one of Vittorio Sella's photographs, 'The Dent du Géant above the Col du Géant, 1881'.

Donkin gave a lecture at the Alpine Club on 28 February 1882 entitled 'High Mountain Photography', which was reprinted in the 1882–84 issue of the *Alpine Journal*. He recorded how he once showed a lady who had never been to Switzerland a photograph of the Gorner Glacier taken from near the châlets above the wood on the way to the Hörnli. Her comment was: 'What a steep road!' 'This remark, however, coming from a person who had never seen a glacier,' he observes, 'does not indicate a lack of perception in the individual so much as a failure on the part of the photograph to represent the facts in their true proportions to the inexperienced eye. It is a matter of common observation that Swiss photographs, of the smaller sizes at least, give scarcely any idea of the mountain and glacier scenes with which we are familiar. Nor is it to be wondered at when we consider how easily the eye is deceived when surveying the scenes themselves: we set off to climb a mountain which looks close at hand, it takes us hours to get to its base; we notice a patch of snow, apparently a few yards wide, up on the rocks above, by the time we get there it has expanded into a snow-field that takes the best part of an hour to cross. After we have laboriously educated the eye to estimate distances in the Alps with some approach to accuracy, we go, say, to Scotland, and allowing ourselves a couple of hours on a misty morning to reach some heathery knoll, we find ourselves on top of it in forty minutes. Perhaps the chief cause of this inaccuracy is what we call atmosphere. Atmosphere, in this technical sense, is an effect produced by watery vapour diffused through the air, which renders details in the distance indistinct and hazy, and we are accustomed to associate distance with haziness. It should be the aim, then, of the photographer of Swiss scenery to give the idea of size and distance by taking advantage of the days when this atmospheric effect is most conspicuous, rather than by choosing those clear days when every detail miles away can be rendered with microscopic sharpness. I do not, however, mean that clearness of detail is incompatible with breadth of effect; on the contrary, one has only to look at the beautiful photographs by Soulier or by England to see that the two may and should coexist. Some have attempted to produce a broad effect in their photographs, by the artifice of leaving the distance a little out of focus, thus rendering the outlines hazy, while bringing the foreground into the sharpest focus; others do just the reverse, leaving the foreground to take care of itself, as in a rough sketch, while giving all the sharpness possible to the distance. But when one looks at a view, the eye unconsciously adjusts its own focus to see with the greatest sharpness that particular portion, whether of far distance or of near foreground, to which it is directed; and since every portion of the picture should be capable of giving the same effect of sharpness of detail when looked at by itself as the corresponding portion of the view, it follows that the whole picture should be sharply in focus. It is in fact by careful attention to the composition and *chiaroscuro* of the picture, not by dodges of focusing, that breadth of effect is to be gained.

'We come now to consider the position of photography in its relation to painting. In the matter of colour, we lose entirely of course all those beautiful effects which are attainable by the painter, and of which we have such excellent examples in our club-rooms. What would be the result of attempting to photograph those lovely effects, seen for a few moments only, but deeply impressed on our memories, as when, for example, we reach the Täsch Alp at early dawn on our way over the Alphubeljoch, and turn round to see the eastern arête of the Weisshorn shining like red gold up in the purple sky? Photography can do nothing with scenes like this; and even when coming down the same path in the afternoon, we find mountain and valley bathed in sunlight, how does the camera represent the sharply defined white pyramid piercing the brilliant blue, and the dark pine-woods and green alps below? In the photograph, the blue sky and white snow are almost indistinguishable, and everything else is nearly black. But although photography is sadly deficient when effects of colour are chiefly concerned, it is in the accurate delineation of form, both in broad outline and in the minutest detail, that it rises pre-eminent. It is therefore among those scenes of rock and snow which depend so little on colour for their accurate representation that the capabilities of photography are turned to the greatest advantage. Conversely, it must be confessed that there are painters who, while representing with marvellous truth the vivid colouring of nature, do sometimes make accuracy of form a minor consideration, the inaccuracy generally being on the side of exaggeration of steepness in mountain forms. How seldom, for example, do we see a painting of the Matterhorn which does not represent it higher and more slender and more pointed than in reality! That there are splendid examples of the exact contrary to this, I should be the last to deny; and if we look at the list of celebrated alpine artists we find that those who best combine accuracy of form with beauty of colouring unite also with those the crowning virtue of being good climbers as well. This tendency to exaggeration is only natural; did we not estimate the steepness of our first snow-slope as being much greater than the reality, and feel decidedly hurt when a scientific companion with a clinometer declared it to be only forty degrees, though we thought it nearly perpendicular?

'But the camera is not liable to such perversions of judgment, and when properly used gives perfectly correct transcripts of form. Whether or not it will also give a representation of the view which will recall the scene to the mind in a satisfactory way, and whether in addition to this the photograph will possess merit as a pictorial composition, depend largely on the skill and artistic perception of the photographer. The question, however, of art in photography scarcely falls within the scope of this paper, and I will only remark that a photographer who can produce a landscape or study which will fully satisfy the rules of composition, is a man to whom the name of artist may well be applied. To get such a picture he must choose his point of view with the utmost care, and having done just this, must wait patiently to seize just the opportunity when the light, the aspect of the sky, and all other circumstances combine to give the fleeting effect which he wants, and which alone will convert his photograph into a picture. However, in photographs of mere rock and snow scenery we do not look for artistic qualities of the highest order—if these are present so much the better—but we value them chiefly as being accurate records of the views . . .

'When I first began photographing in Switzerland in 1877, I used small plates, 5×4 inches, and a light camera and stand, with three double slides holding two plates each, the whole apparatus, including a sling case, weighing only about 7 lbs. Photographs of this small size, however, are rather insignificant in appearance, and in 1879 I took out a larger kit, suitable for 7½×5-inch plates. Finding occasionally that a supply of six plates was insufficient for long expeditions, in the following year I further increased my impedimenta by adopting a new arrangement for carrying the sensitive plates, known as Hare's changing box; it holds twelve plates, any one of which can be transferred to a slide, exposed in the camera, and returned to the box without any possibility of extraneous light reaching it. The whole apparatus, packed in a leather knapsack, weighed about 18 lbs and the tripod stand 3 lbs more, packed on the top of the knapsack. . . . Most climbers prefer to carry as little as possible themselves; against this I must set the pleasure of complete independence, so that one can ramble about with one's camera entirely alone, without either hiring a porter or boring one's companions.

'The circumstances, indeed, of an arrival on top of a mountain on a brilliant morning, with a glorious view all round, and with a very limited time to spend there, are somewhat at variance with the cool deliberation requisite in order to make no mistakes while setting up the apparatus and going through the necessary series of operations, the omission of any of which may spoil the result. I did, in fact, lose the first four of the plates I took up the Weisshorn through inattention to one adjustment of the camera . . .

'Still, a small photograph well taken and nicely mounted may be a charming little object, and much better than none at all, whatever one may say against it theoretically. Of course no photograph can equal a really good sketch, but to sketch well and rapidly is far more difficult than to take a good photograph. The wish must have occurred to most climbers to have the power of bringing home with them some record, however imperfect, of the scenery they pass through. To all such who cannot sketch I would say, take up photography; do not be deterred by the dry details and apparent difficulties on which I have perhaps dilated too long in this paper, but which are easily surmounted. Those members of the club and others who have already taken it up will, I am sure, bear me out in saying that photography combined with mountaineering is a most fascinating and delightful pursuit.'

We can see how, during the ninety years since Donkin's lecture, the reproduction machine, as we may well call the camera, has developed and reached mechanical perfection. In the imaginative approach, however, in the capture of the reality, in the artistic framework of the picture taken, indeed in the whole spiritual world of photography, there has been hardly a single step forward.

The first British photographer to climb Mont Blanc from the Col Emil Rey by the Brouillard Ridge was H. O. Jones on 9 September 1911. He left photographs of this first ascent and from the Dent du Géant. In the following year he and his young bride were killed on the Aiguille Noire de Peuterey.

Prof. Wilhelm Paulcke, the pioneer of skiing and winter-photography, published his picture 'On the Valluga summit, 13 March 1902' in the Austrian Alpenverein journal. He fought hard with his written accounts and his photographs to further the cause of high-mountain skiing. Alfred Asal's picture 'The downhill run' in the 1924 *Alpenfreund* is one of the first photographs to capture the dynamic motion of skiing. As cameras were perfected and the sensitivity of films improved, the ability to take a sharp picture of rapid movement gradually increased.

An enormous photographic panorama of the view from the Gornergrat above Zermatt was made for the World Exposition in St Louis, USA, in 1904. This 'finest panorama in the world', as it came to be known, consisted of sections taken on 7×9-inch negatives. The finished enlargement measured 67 ft $\times$ 6 ft 9 in.

General Theodor von Wundt (d. 1929) was a keen climber, one of the first winter-alpinists and an outstanding photographer; he was the first to publish really excellent pictures taken on very difficult climbs. His picture-books *The Ascent of the Cimone della Pala: An Album for Climbers and Dolomite Addicts* (1890) and *Rambles in the Ampezzo Dolomites* (1893) contributed much to the popularity of rock-climbing by the interest and liveliness of their pictures.

Wundt complained in his book *The Mountains and I—A Wanderer's Life* that in 1884, on his first winter tour in the High Tatra, he had already regretted his total inability to capture 'the separate impressions of the magnificence of the landscape in winter. That made me decide,' he wrote, 'to throw myself heart and soul into photography, which had just at that moment made a great stride forward owing to the discovery of dry plates, making it possible to take pictures outside a studio. There were practically no amateur photographers then and the difficulties, particularly in high-mountain photography, were immense. That, however, added to the fun, and I hoped to be able to get somewhere aided by a degree of inventiveness and a bit of fiddling. It is almost impossible to describe the trials I had to endure, but this only spurred me on to a boundless enthusiasm. To start with, I walked myself flat-footed under the unbearable weight of glass plates; then I worked my way through negative paper, stripping-films and gelatine-films which, quite apart from their various unsatisfactory features, carried a different factor of sensitivity every year; and I don't know how many cameras I made. Everything you buy ready-made in a shop nowadays had to be invented, constructed and brought into being at the cost of endless labour and great expense. Then, after the next tour, you had to start all over again, because it had resulted in entirely fresh attitudes.'

Otto Melzer of Innsbruck, who fell to his death with his friend Emil Spötl on 6 October 1901, while climbing the north face of the Praxmarerkarspitze in the Karwendel, was an enthusiastic photographer who tried throughout his life to reproduce the beauty of the Alps. He was always bent on doing still better, on setting higher standards. He often took pictures on the hardest pitches of his climbs, in order to get the most impressive and revealing photographs possible. They gave the Face on which he died his name—the Melzerwand.

After his death, a book called *Masterpieces from the Tyrolese Alps: Among Innsbruck's Mountains* was published, consisting of his own original photographs and a text by Heinrich von Ficker. The photographer takes us with him into his mountain homeland through a series of exquisitely reproduced copper-plate heliogravures. His friend Ficker wrote: 'Few knew the name of Otto Melzer. Yet no better man ever roved our homeland hills, none ever knew them better, even if others may have climbed more summits. He knew them, too, in all their loveliness; and because his whole soul was devoted to them with a deep, ardent love, he also tried to lead others along the path leading to that world of surpassing beauty.'

A great step forward for mountain photography resulted from the setting up at Leipzig in 1908 of an 'Alpine Clubs' Centre for collecting lantern-slides'. The size of the diapositives for this representative collection of contemporary slides was fixed at $3\frac{3}{4} \times 4\frac{3}{4}$ inches.

Dr Anton Mazel's book *Artistic Mountain Photography* appeared in Berlin during the same year. The author, president of the Geneva Photographic Society and a member of the Swiss Alpine Club, stated that 'an artist, in order to render the mountains in their true poetry, must visualize them with the eye of an eagle'. The club's yearbook for 1910 contained a paper by Dr Gustav A. Kuhfahl on 'Photography in the Alps'. Another work of his, *High Mountain and Winter Photography*, achieved a seventh edition at Halle on the Saale in 1928.

Dr Arnold Fanck (born in 1889) was a passionate mountain-lover. In 1913 he produced the first skiing film taken among high mountains: its subject, his first ascent of Monte Rosa

(15,217 feet) on skis. His later associates were the camera-man Sepp Allgeier, who published a book, *The Hunt for a Picture—18 years as a Camera-man in the Arctic and High Mountains* (1931), and Luis Trenker, whom Fanck converted from a fine climber into a famous film-star. Hannes Schneider, too (1890–1955), the skiing wonder from the Arlberg, who introduced skiing into the Far East (*Japan on Skis*) was a pupil of Fanck's.

Dr Fanck's films were *Snowshoe Marvels* (part 1—1919, part 2—1922), *Man against the Mountains* (1921), *The Holy Mountain* (1924), *The White Hell of Piz Palü* (1928–9), *Storms over Mont Blanc* (1930), *The White Cataract* (1931) and *The Ultimate Dream, the First Ascent of Mont Blanc* (1934). In 1924 he published his instructional book *Snowshoe Marvels*, laying down the basic approach to skiing technique. In that comprehensive work he included many single frames out of strips taken from his masterly skiing films. The method is strongly reminiscent of the motion studies of men and horses published by the English photographer Edward Muybridge in 1877. Just as he captured the actual movements of a galloping horse in his photographs, so Fanck caught the motions of a skier, as he runs downhill leaving a powdery haze of snow behind him, in a series of minutely-detailed pictures. The presence of the perforations in the printed version was definite evidence of their origin as film-strips. By studying the representations of the correct positions the beginner could thus learn the 'white art' more rapidly. In his *Animal Locomotion: Electro-photographic Investigations of Consecutive Phases of Animal Movement*, Muybridge used a dynamic series of more than 20,000 photographs of those phases. It is very possible that Fanck took as his prototype these 'progressive series', which aroused as much admiration among artists and photographers as had the Pattern-books of the Middle Ages hundreds of years earlier. Fanck's *Ski-runner's Picture Book*, containing 284 superb cine-shots, appeared in 1932. His life was devoted to reproducing man's existence in the setting of high mountains and nature's winter garb. In his pictures he strove to represent, above all else, movement.

The mountain-film *The Blue Light*, directed by Leni Riefenstahl in 1932, was a film-play based on an old legend of the Dolomites. Monte Cristallo has a marvellous blue sheen in moonlight. That sheen lured the young villagers from the foot of the mountain on to its rocky face, out of sheer love of adventure, inquisitiveness or the greedy hope of hidden treasure. Time and again they fell to their death in the gulfs below. Later on a painter discovered that the mysterious blue light radiated from a cave in the rock of the mountain, lined with massive rock-crystals, which reflect the light of the moon. The inhabitants of the village plunder this treasure-house of crystal and become rich on the proceeds.

The Blue Light left the observer with the sorrowful recognition that the world, stripped of its magic, where a miracle turns to a commercial gimmick, can only mean a spiritual loss to mankind. The last message of the film to the man of today was that when no magic light is any longer tolerated on the peaks, all feeling for the beauty of elemental nature must perish —just as Junta the gypsy girl, who represents the elemental forces in the film, falls to her death from the Cristallo's face as she climbs to rob the crystal cave of its treasure. The film, which was shot just at the end of the era of the silent film, was impressive for the truth and reality with which it represented the typical peasants of the Sarntal.

In the film *Flags on the Matterhorn* (1928) Luis Trenker, also famous for his films, worked alongside Sepp Allgeier as director and producer. Trenker's first film in his own right was the highly successful *Son of the White Mountains* (1930). In his alpine film-drama *Mountains in Flames* (1931) his theme was the experiences of troops engaged in high-mountain warfare in the South Tyrol and included a fantastic skiing sequence, when a Tyrolese officer ran down to visit his native village, occupied by the enemy. Man and his fate were Trenker's main motif, set in the framework of nature's magnificence. Ernst Baumann of Bad Reichenhall was Trenker's chief camera-man for a long time; this 'virtuoso of the Rolleiflex' demanded of a good photograph that 'it should tell a story'.

Marcel Ichac shot several high-mountain films of a high standard: *4100* (1934), *Karakorum* (1936), *The Assault on the Aiguilles du Diable* (1942), *The Conquest of Annapurna* (1950–2), and *Starlight at Noon* (1959). More recently Gaston Rebuffat and Georges Tairraz have made a name together in *Starlight and Storms* (1955) and *Between Earth and Sky* (1961).

The Englishman Tom Stobart will always be remembered for his epoch-making film of the successful British climb of Everest in 1953.

Luigi Ghedina, a Dolomite photographer resident in Cortina d'Ampezzo, took fascinatingly beautiful pictures, particularly in South Tyrol. Between the wars, André Roch, the Swiss climber, illustrated the icy world of the peaks between Orsières and Saas Fée and the sublime beauty of the Western Alps in his *The World of the Haute-Route Summits*. His picture book, *Classic Climbs in the Alps*, consists entirely of his own pictures. In St Moritz, Albert Steiner was one of the first among modern photographers to aim at sheer beauty of scene in his mountain pictures, using a large plate-camera to render the loveliness of the mountains, eschewing all cheap effects. Dr Adalbert Defner of Igls near Innsbruck, whose effective pictures have been widely sold for several decades as attractive postcards, had the gift of avoiding all gimmicks. He was perhaps the last to record the surpassingly beautiful landscape of the Tyrol while it was yet unspoilt.

The history of the Leitz camera, the Leica, was of the utmost importance for climbers, as the forerunner of the miniature camera which has been so fully developed through the last few decades. Oskar Barnack, who invented it, was a keen photographic enthusiast. He was well aware that only large pictures give a natural impression to the viewer, because it is only when the beholder can see it from a satisfactory distance that his eyes can enjoy the full impact and message of the picture. But could one go on carting heavy great cameras and their accessories on walking- or climbing-tours with all the encumbrance entailed? Clearly climbers required a small but serviceable camera. It was Barnack who seized upon the notion of the 'big picture from the small camera' and it brought him world fame. The duplication in size of cine-film from 18×24 mm to 24×36 mm was the basis for the idea of the Leica-film so long essential. The miniature film spread like wild-fire; it had, of course, all the advantages of cine-film—small grain, cheapness following on mass-production, world-wide distribution, the ability to transport it in the camera and the feature that the perforation kept it flat at all times. The Leica was first marketed in 1925. The first alpine Leica picture-book, Dr Paul Wolff's *Ski-companion Toni*, came out in the following year, consisting of action pictures and snapshots.

Prof. Stefan Kruckenhauser, who gave us wonderful pictures of the skiing world round about St Christoph in the *Austrian Manual of Ski-Instruction*, wrote: 'It would be far better if we went around more. One can never find the true beauty of the landscape if one does not explore it with one's eyes open!' In his illustrated text-book, *The Lovely Tyrolese Winter: Experiences on Skis and Among the High Mountains with a Leica* (Berlin, 1937), he commented: 'The old hunting proverb, of which Hannes Schneider once reminded me when I was nosing round like a dachshund in the snow with my camera, holds equally true in photography: "there is more game put up than run down".'

One of the most important photographers between the two World Wars was the Englishman Frank Smythe, who produced a number of picture-books of the Alps, the Rockies and other ranges. Smythe went on to take superb photographs up to 28,000 feet on Everest, and was certainly one of the outstanding mountaineers and mountain photographers of our time. Another eminent photographer of the Alps, the Dolomites, rock-climbing in general and the mountain scene, is C. Douglas Milner, with several splendid books to his credit. W. F. Poucher is also well known for a lifetime of photography among the British hills, Scotland, Wales and the Lakes (where he has never had a rival), and also in the Alps.

An extraordinary book of Everest photography was produced as a result of the team effort of André Roch, Raymond Lambert and Norman Dyhrenfurt, on the occasion of the two unsuccessful Swiss attempts on the peak in 1952. The American Norman Dyhrenfurt was also responsible for the wonderful picture-book of the American Everest expedition which made the first traverse in 1963. In addition, he shot a magnificent film of the enterprise.

Heinz Müller-Bruncke (of Grassau in the Chiemgau) provided much practical experience and little theorizing in his book *Mountain Photography* (1958). He was ideally suited to mountain photography, for it was a combination of love for the mountain world and picture-making which led to his successful career. In a book called *Photo-hunter in the Snow*, Lothar Rübelt of Vienna gave many useful hints for winter landscape photography and for avoiding errors when taking pictures of winter-sports scenes. Other well-known and talented landscape- and mountain-photographers are Robert Löbl (Bad Tölz), Risch-Lau (Bregenz) and Vilem Heckel, one of the leading alpine photographers in East Europe, with his fine pictures of movement, depicting 'the little man among the big mountains' as his theme.

Kurt Diemberger of Salzburg is possibly the greatest living Austrian mountaineer, and the only man to have stood on the summit of two 'Eight Thousanders'. He is a first-class photographer of the Himalayan and Karakorum giants; his sunset photograph from the 26,600-foot summit of 'Broad Peak' is world famous and probably the finest alpine photograph ever taken. His summit panorama from the same point is of unsurpassed scientific as well as scenic interest. He has photographed in the Alps, Corsica and the Hindu Kush, in colour and black-and-white, with a real mountain artist's eye. His film *Peuterey Ridge of Mont Blanc* is a valuable record of that huge six-day climb.

The German Erwin Schneider ranks as the most prolific and universal of this century's great alpine climber-photographers, on whose incomparable collection almost every author of mountaineering books has relied for illustrations. He has lived in South America for many years. In very recent years, Dr Walter Kirstein, a fine mountaineer and member of the Alpine Club, has been prominent in colour and black-and-white. Others of note are Basil Goodfellow, Christian Bonington and Hugh Merrick.

In Walter Pause's picture-book *The Alps Through an Eagle's Eyes* (Munich, 1966), Franz Thorbecke's starkly graphic black-and-white pictures discover the mountains through a 'totally new' bird's-eye optical technique. It is impossible to take pleasure in these pictures without reservations and regrets; for in them there is nothing of the mountains left to the imagination any more. Every last primeval cranny lies revealed, thanks to the unfettered technical media employed. The stripping of the mountains of their secrets robs them of any sense of excitement and suspense, of their mysterious element and of the unseen surprises round the corner. At the end of twenty centuries there is nothing new for man to discover. The claim that 'the false perspective from above or below has been overcome' is fallacious. Apparently the technocrat-photographer can only succeed from the comfort of his aircraft. But the mountain landscape can only reveal itself in its human perspective to men whose eyes are open to perceive it while walking, scrambling, climbing. And another, and unpleasant, result of this 'new, surprising mountain experience' is the penetrating disturbance of the quiet mountain regions by the din of ever more and more aircraft. Moreover, many decades ago, photographers had already succeeded in seeing and capturing the mountains 'from above' (though in blessed silence!). In the D.Ö.A. Journal of 1927 Dr Robert Liefmann wrote an account of 'Alpine Flights in a Balloon', illustrated by very good bird's-eye photography. In the same publication Margarete Grosse wrote about 'Ballooning over the Alps' in 1911; she revealed that the first trans-alpine balloon flight had happened by accident to the French balloonist Arban in the mid-nineteenth century, when he was carried away by a gale across the Maritime Alps from Marseilles and landed at Turin next day. The first intentional big venture by balloon was undertaken by a Swiss, Eduard Spelterini, who ascended from Sion on an alpine flight on 3 October 1898.

It is only natural that the camera went along to the summit of the Eight-Thousanders when the time came for the world's last great climbs. Annapurna, the first of the fourteen great peaks of over the 8,000-metre level—all in the Himalayas or the Karakorum—to be climbed, was the scene of a tragedy brought about by photography. On 2 June 1950 a party of French climbers reached its summit. Up there, that fateful morning, which had unveiled yet another of the world's secrets, Maurice Herzog, the leader of the expedition, took some pictures. Without thinking, he took off his gloves, which were hampering him. Affected by the lack of oxygen at so great an altitude, he failed to notice the loss of protection to his hands, which was absolutely essential in the paralysing cold, and was so badly frostbitten that they both had to be amputated. And the worst of it is that the summit pictures, taken at such a cost, were lost in a crevasse on that terrible descent.

In 1953 Colonel Hunt's British team was the first to reach the summit of 'Peak XV' (29,028 feet), the designation given in 1852 by an officer of the Survey of India, who discovered it, to the world's highest peak, later christened Mount Everest in honour of an earlier Surveyor General. On 29 May 1953 Edmund P. Hillary, a New Zealander, and the Sirdar of Sherpas Tenzing Norkay got to the top, so registering the ultimate high triumph in the long line of attempts and successes in pushing up the altitude record among the world's great peaks. The historic moment was immortalized by the camera. In spite of their great exhaustion, the successful pair took a number of photographs, which are there for all to see: at once a documentation and a confirmation of that tremendous achievement.

212

'The eye is the window of the soul'
LEONARDO DA VINCI

Vittorio Sella (1859–1943) was a great mountaineer. He made a winter traverse of Mont Blanc between 31 December 1887 and 6 January 1888, and visited the Caucasus, Himalaya, Alaska and Africa. Above all, he was the man who led the nascent art of mountain photography to its highest flights. Some of his Himalayan pictures remain unsurpassed today. Plate 213 (Mont Blanc from above the Col du Géant) was taken by him as long ago as 1880! Plate 212 shows him in 1909.

213

Mountain photography used to be hard work indeed. Apart from the heavy equipment, a tent had to be taken along in which the photographer prepared his plates beforehand and then developed them immediately after taking the picture (Plate 215).

Filming in the mountains is still a job for 'tough guys', even if downpours are staged with a bucket of water. Plate 216 was among the frames of Lothar Brandler's *A European Rope*. A veritable film-expedition was necessary to shoot the hair-raising pictures of the 'Swiss Route' on the north face of the Western Zinne, which turned his film *Alpine Sensation* in 1966 into an actual one (Plate 217 shows the camera-team in a bivouac).

Long ago, when climbers wanted to be photographed, the photographer started by putting up a suitable back-cloth, enhanced by a few stones in the foreground to provide the mountain atmosphere. Plate 214 shows a gathering of famous climbers and guides: seated, the British climbers J. S. Phillimore and A. G. Rayner, who were the first to master the mighty face of the Civetta. Standing, Giuseppe Colli and Antonio Dimai (first up the south face of the Tofana). Kneeling, Angelo Dibona (north face of the Einser, Laliderer north face, etc.).

215

◂ 214

216

217

The pioneers of mountain photography always took their cameras along. They were fanatics, sparing neither themselves nor anyone else, witness the seven climbers on a sérac in the Mont Blanc Range (Plate 218). One wonders how long the poor devils had to hold their poses while a photographer of the day took his picture in 1880? Vittorio Sella's camera was on hand, too, when the Queen of Italy climbed Monte Rosa for the opening of the Capanna Margherita. A contemporary of Sella's was Fritz Benesch (1868–1949, shown in Plate 220 a year before his death), one of the outstanding mountain photographers of the day. In 1894 he made the first ascent of the Dent de Mesdi in the Dolomites and later he led a photographic expedition to the peak. Here is his description of how he took Plate 221: 'I went cautiously up a short chimney of brittle rock to the notch behind the pillar, then reached up, put my arms around the top of the rock and pulled myself up onto my airy perch. I found myself stuck like a fly on the tip of the rock-finger and for a long time sat looking around me and down into the depths, turn by turn, over and over again, before I dared to move. My uneven seat measured little more than a foot square. I managed somehow to open my tripod, but my chief headache was where to position myself. At my request, the two men straddled on the notch below passed the pieces of equipment to me, one after another. In this way, while still sitting, I built the tripod up above me, then screwed the box and the lenses to it, until everything was in place down to the last detail. Then it was my turn to exercise my own talents, which would have got me a job anywhere as a contortionist: all that was required of me was to crawl out from underneath without touching anything, knocking anything off into the abyss and, last but not least, without myself falling off.'

220

◀ 218

219 ▼

221

The Austrian Alpine Club's photographic competitions. The adjudicators sit for days looking at a mountain photograph before reaching a decision. We reproduce the first three prize-winners in the competitions held respectively in 1964, 1965 and 1966.

1964. 1st Prize, Peter Mangutsch of Innsbruck's 'Battle Zone'; 2nd Prize, Toni Kohler of Lustenau's 'Up into the Sky'; 3rd Prize, Leopold Pahitsch of Vienna's 'November Mists'.

1965. 1st Prize, Andreas Schandert of Staudach's 'The Way to the Light'; 2nd Prize, Eduard Kargel of Villach's 'The Awakening of the Wischberg'; 3rd Prize, Karl Kolar of Vienna's 'Every day is like a short year – the Gjaidsteinsattel on the Dachstein'.

1966. 1st Prize, Wilhelm Maresch of Bad Goisern's 'The Mowers'; 2nd Prize, Erich Vejvar of Maria Enzersdorf's 'Out of Darkness into Light'; 3rd Prize, Karl Meusberger of Hirschegg's 'First Light'.

1964/1

1965/1

1964/2

1964/3

1966/1

1965/2

1966/2

1965/3

1966/3

The Grandes Jorasses (13,799 ft) is a mighty peak and its north face a mighty wall.

Recently, Bradford Washburn, an American, has attracted widespread acclaim for his remarkable (aerial) photographs which are being reproduced in numerous alpine publications. Right: his 'The Grandes Jorasses' with the moon above its towering precipices (Plate 231).

Professional and amateur. Heinz Müller-Brunke, born in Berlin, is a photographer by profession and an enthusiastic mountain-photographer. His pictures enshrine what everyone is seeking, heart and soul, in the mountains. His picture (Plate 233) is entitled 'The old peasants' path to the Schlern'.

Adi Mokrejs is an amateur, who never takes a step in the hills without his camera. Even on difficult rock-climbs he is always on the look-out for subjects. He calls Plate 232 'A World of Rock'. It shows the smooth slabs of the west face of the Fleischbank in the Wilde Kaiser (Kaisergebirge). When he took the picture he was engaged on the climb of the Predigtstuhl's north arête.

232, 233

Mountain streams provide some of the most satisfactory subjects for the alpine photographer. There is good reason why the directors of the classical mountain films repeatedly showed mountain lakes and waterfalls. They knew what an effect these had on their audiences. These two pictures were taken by Pedrotti, the photographer from Trento.

234, 235 ▸

The classic mountain films. It took Arnold Fanck, the film-director, a year and a half to put together his film 'The Holy Mountain'. First shown in 1926, it still remains among the ten best mountain films ever shot. Fanck had a passion for light and shadow, and originated the 'artistic mountain film'. Plates 236 and 237 give some idea of the beauty of his film, which can still enthrall the viewer.

Luis Trenker's films have quite a different appeal. They rely on power, action, the atmosphere of the climb. Director and actor, Trenker knew his mountains like the back of his hand. During the shooting of his film 'The Mountain Calls', he drove his camera-team, carrying loads of 50 lbs and more, from the Hörnli Hut to the top of the Matterhorn in precisely four hours. Some of his pictures have become historic. Reproduced here are shots from 'The Struggle for the Matterhorn' and 'Mountains in Flames' (Plates 239 and 238).

The modern mountain-film has reverted to the search for the pictorial, more especially the pictorially unusual. The picture overleaf, on the last page of the book, is taken from Jürgen Görter's film 'Grade VI on Skis'.

◀ 236 237 ▲ 238 239

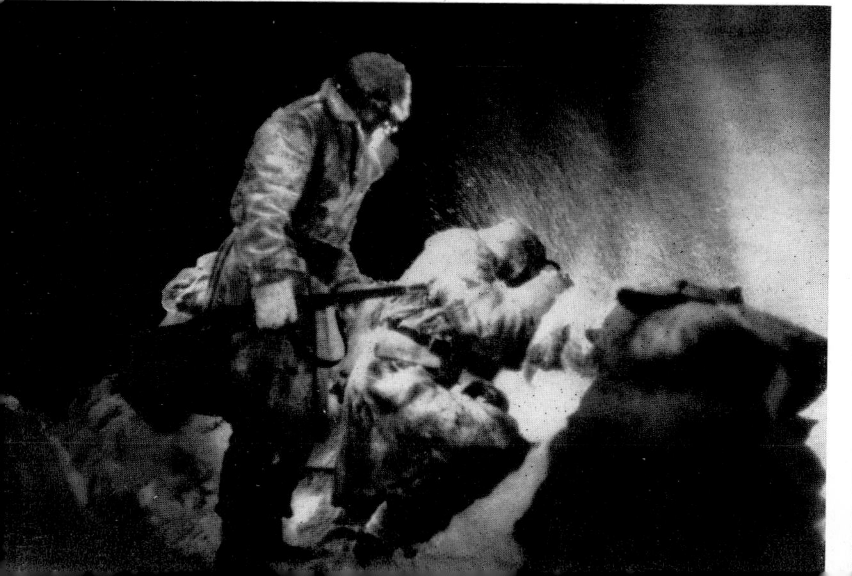